INNOVATING INNOVATION!

INNOVATING INNOVATION!

WHY CORPORATE INNOVATION STRUGGLES IN THE AGE OF THE ENTREPRENEUR

MIKE STEMPLE

I N S P I R E R
PUBLISHING

INNOVATING INNOVATION!
Why Corporate Innovation Struggles in the Age of the Entrepreneur

ISBN   978-0-9996025-3-9   *Paperback*
        978-0-9996025-2-2   *Ebook*
        978-0-9996025-4-6   *Audiobook*

For Nina.

CONTENTS

INTRODUCTION

"You suck at innovation."

I unfortunately have to tell corporations this all the time.

Why is it that a corporate employee can come up with an innovative idea and get nowhere with it? Despite having an abundance of resources, the corporate innovator is often left begging for time, talent, and treasure. Why is it that this same employee can quit their job, found a startup, and be wildly successful as an entrepreneur—with the same idea?

There has never been a better moment in history to be an entrepreneur than right now. The nature of innovation today encourages nimbleness, flexibility, and creativity above all else. It's an exciting time to be an innovator. For those same reasons, it's a drain to be stuck in a traditionally structured business.

So here's the big question: why do big companies suck at innovation?

First, I tell them it's not their fault. They are trapped in an antiquated way of innovating that hasn't responded to the evolution that has happened to innovation. Innovation itself has evolved. Technology has become democratized, talent costs less, time investment has shrunk.

The reason why corporations are failing is because they are not thinking and acting like a startup.

When I sit down with CEOs who have hired me as a consultant, I make it clear that they might individually be a talented innovator, but their business lags behind. More often than not, their company is hostile to modern "innovation," despite their marketing and branding using the word (incorrectly) all the time. Most of the companies I work with spend millions of dollars innovating because they conceptually know it's important, but they don't understand why they do it.

When I ask corporate leaders why they're spending so much on innovation and what it is that they're trying to evolve into or develop, they usually have a hard time answering the question. This is because companies are good at staying the same and bad at changing. An "innovation department" within a traditional business won't be able to do anything beyond the limitations of its structure.

Innovators, by our very nature, challenge stability, question it, tweak it: we make things better through change. We take losses one quarter to experiment so that we can double, triple, or quadruple our profits the next with something truly disruptive. It is the innovator's job to cut away what doesn't work, enhance the things that do, and fill in the gaps with the new and radical.

Reasonably, this makes most operational leaders very anxious. That's why there are so few innovators leading larger organizations; the people in charge of hiring innovators are ideologically opposed to them.

That's why so many innovators leave large organizations to build their own startups.

That's why so many companies suck at innovation.

YOU'RE HIRING THE WRONG PEOPLE

Big companies are losing to startups in one other key area: talent.

The problem starts in Human Resources (HR). Most hiring departments are operating on a two-decades-old paradigm. In this mindset, third-party qualification is the most important thing. Certifications, degrees, references—these are the things that get you hired by outdated HR departments. Meanwhile, first-party qualification—actual ability to do the job, efficiency, culture-fit—are considered secondary, things to only be taken into consideration once the MBA or other worthless degree box has been checked.

The result: hiring departments with no guarantees that they will bring in people who can do what they were hired for.

Most of the companies I work with would never hire me. They'll bring me on as a consultant to help them run their business, but their HR departments would see my lack of certifications and the amount that I bounce between businesses as a problem; in reality, these are my skill sets, the very reasons why I'm hired to work for massive corporations around the country. What makes me an asset as a consultant to today's company is precisely what makes me a liability to most HR departments' hiring practices—which were created twenty years ago.

Corporations will pass on Picasso just to end up with Paul the accountant. Their HR departments prioritize stable operators over entrepreneurial innovators. This is why so many companies can't innovate: they don't have any innovators in their organization.

If a big company manages to hire innovators, they struggle to keep them. Every year, traditional companies lose their best employees to startups. Even worse, the people who leave those companies tend to start businesses that directly compete with their previous employers. Big companies have effectively created a pipeline from their onboarding programs to their direct competitors.

Based on a November 2021 survey of 8,000 U.S. employees, commissioned by QuickBooks, 57 percent want to start their own business. One in five of them will actually found a startup. If that number holds true across the country, that means there will be 5 million EINs (Employer Identification Number) generated in 2022 alone.[1] The less large companies do to compete, the more that number will rise.

It's not hard to see why so many people want to go out on their own. As part of my work as an innovation consultant, I attend a lot of in-house innovation events run by large corporations. After these events, I ask the employees if they feel able to innovate in their jobs. More importantly, I ask if

---

1   Simon Worsfold, "New Business Insights: 2022 Projected to Be Another Record Year for New Business Starts," *QuickBooks Blog*, December 20, 2021, https://quickbooks.intuit.com/r/inspiration/new-business-insights-dec-2021/.

they're excited to innovate or how they feel about their work. Almost every time, these employees will tell me that they either aren't innovating or they are completely apathetic to the innovation their company wants them to do.

Big companies have droves of talented employees working in jobs where they feel stifled, where they feel like they can't bring their best ideas to the table and have them implemented. With so much money floating around in the startup space, it's surprising that only 57 percent of US employees want to start their own business.

In an innovation economy, startups dominate the money and talent pool. Big companies are dying a death by a thousand cuts while their best employees leave to found businesses that eat their profits. Operating as they have been for the last decades or so, large corporations will continue to flounder and fail until startups begin to acquire them.

The solutions are obvious, though many companies don't want to hear them. In order to respond to contemporary innovation, companies need to do four things.

HOW TO DO BETTER

Humans are predisposed to innovate. That's how our brains work: we see patterns, notice what doesn't fit in, and try to make sense of the chaos. It's natural for us to reassess and reevaluate, to expand our ways of thinking. Because so many companies fear change, they never innovate. In essence, big companies deny their people the chance to be human, to do what they do best.

If you want to bring true innovators into your business, and if you don't want to lose the top-people you have, you need to do four things. Every chapter of this book will help you do one or more of them.

Focus on talent. People are the heart of any business. It's not enough to just hire talented people; you have to take care of them and let them be human. High-performance individuals will do well only if you let them.

Act more like a startup. Startups tell great stories. They inspire people. They lead with vision over facts. That's how they get the best people and the most money. Startups also move quickly and nimbly; they are able to respond to the evolution of innovation. The more you can make your business like a startup, the better positioned you'll be to take every opportunity that comes along.

Get out of your own way. Process and operations are overrated. Too many companies get bogged in *how* they do things that they stop to ask *how well* they do them. Performance beats process every time. This goes back to the first point.

If you let your people do things the way that they do them best, you won't need to waste any time creating convoluted processes.

Find the treasure. Money isn't trivial. A startup with a smart team can get more money and more liquid funds than the largest corporations. Investors want to be told a great story and to be inspired. No matter how great your product or service is, if you're not packaging it in an appealing, dynamic way to investors, you'll leave huge stores of money on the table. Go where the money is and create a plan to get it.

WHY YOU BOUGHT THIS BOOK

Learning about innovation is challenging. "Innovation" has become such a buzzword that it's hard to know what you're getting into before reading a book or attending a conference on the topic. Most people don't know what they're talking about and completely misuse the word.

What you need to know about innovation, however, is simple.

As you read this book, you'll understand what innovation actually is and how to communicate its value across your company. You'll develop a common lexicon of innovation that you and your team can use to make a better product, run a more efficient business, and stay competitive with the thousands of startups that are challenging you from all sides.

You'll realize that you need to make dramatic changes. As you already learned, innovation is risky. If you are serious about shaking up your company, you need to make changes—innovations—that shake things up. This might be uncomfortable, but that's how you'll know you're doing what you need to. No matter how scary it might feel, evolving your business is infinitely less frightening than watching it die a slow death.

You'll learn how the lack of innovation condenses people into a tight, predictable, manageable mode; basically, it makes people drones not thinkers. Innovation isn't just a product or end goal—it's a process that unlocks the creativity and ingenuity of your people. You'll see how stability and rigidity undermine your efforts and how dynamism and fluidity position your company to succeed.

Lastly, you'll know what you need to get rid of in order to create real innovation: hierarchy. Only when there are no rules and no oppressive structures in place can you solely focus on pleasing your consumer. That's how you'll get your company back to a founder mindset, back to an entrepreneurial spirit that will help you weather the contemporary world. If you want to dominate your market, you have to abolish hierarchies.

WHO I AM

I'm not an MBA. I'm ex-military. I was a combat medic in the US Army straight out of high school. My background is in psychology. At one point, I wanted to go to medical school. In my twenties, I suffered a brain injury that unlocked the art center of my brain. I became hyper-creative, curious, and innovative. The scientist and the artist in me combined to become a successful serial internet entrepreneur. When I got tired of that, I became an athlete, racing across deserts all over the world. These experiences give me a unique perspective to look at the world.

I work with some of the biggest and best companies in the world now. I use my singular background to show them things they can't see on their own, that their traditional mindsets won't reveal.

I have founded dozens of startups from scratch, all from my own original ideas. Some of them became successful, some of them became *really* successful, and most failed. And that's okay; the way to my success is always through my failures.

I've had multiple careers where I have ended up in the top 1 percent of my field. There is one reason why I always end up at the top—no matter the industry, time, or place. That one reason is that I embrace change. I use failure, seek it out, and craft it into value. I welcome risk, let it teach me everything it knows. I think like an entrepreneur.

I am one thing that most innovation consultants in this space aren't: a genuine innovator. Read this book and you'll understand contemporary innovation better.

This book isn't like other popular books on innovation, written by academics who have only observed others who innovate. This book will provide you with one of two outcomes; either it will help you understand contemporary innovation and implement the newer ways of building innovations, or it will inspire you to take the journey I did and go out and build your own innovations without the antiquated restraints to which dying big businesses are clinging.

Once you internalize these concepts, you will be able to chase true innovation. That hunt will take your company places you never thought it could go.

CHAPTER 1

DEFINING INNOVATION

There are so many craft beers that you could drink a different craft beer every day for the rest of your life and still not have tried them all. I was consulting at a multinational beverage company when I witnessed an example of slow but steady damage to this company's market share. Big breweries were so worried about what the other big guys were doing that they failed to recognize or respond to the threats posed by the burgeoning craft beer industry. Any one brand of craft beer had no chance of hurting the big beer producers, so it was easy to dismiss the threat entirely. But when taken in totality, each one of those thousands of small brands is selling against these large incumbents, creating a massive disruption. Corporations fail to understand that it's not Anheuser-Busch versus Heineken. It's Budweiser versus thousands of microbreweries from around the globe. And each and every one of those dismissed craft brewers are innovating without the bureaucracy and legacy that is endemic within large corporations. Any one of the tens of thousands of full-time innovators around the globe could create the "next big thing" that steals millions from the entrenched multinationals. And yet, because they are singularly small, they are dismissed, even though in innovation, big things have small beginnings.

In a sense, innovation is a company's immune system, a way of successfully responding to market changes and emerging threats. People tend to focus on existential threats that could kill a company entirely, but these massive, problematic threats are rare. A company is far more likely to die by a thousand cuts—repeatedly failing to respond to the plethora of small threats, especially the threats posed by truly innovative startups. It is this legion of innovators that are attacking and killing large companies.

Another threat is the term "innovation" itself, which is one of the most overused and misunderstood words in corporations, both large and small. The word itself has been corrupted by personal agenda and incorrect usage to the extent that no one seems to know what it means anymore. If we are going to *honestly* tackle the problem of innovation in business today, we need a precise definition of innovation.

In my years of experience as an Entrepreneur in Residence (EIR), I have seen the term misused across all departments within companies and across various industries. Here are some direct quotes that illustrate the kind of confusion caused by the many different definitions in everyday use:

- CEOs pitch to the market that they have a "culture of **innovation**" and that "**innovation** is our primary focus."

- Technology teams use it as a goal: "We need to be more **innovative**."

- Sales teams use it as a competitive differentiator: "This is the most **innovative** product."

- Operations teams use it as a goal: "**Innovative** efficiencies in the supply chain."

- Human Resources uses the term to recruit new talent: "Come work for us. We are an **innovative** company."

- Marketing teams use it as a slogan: "We are **innovative**."

In the examples above, each department puts its own spin on the term. Unfortunately, the various meanings and personal agendas only muddy the waters. The term "innovation" cannot be used in so many different ways and remain a consistent, coherent concept.

Returning to the dictionary itself for a definition of "innovation" reveals something that a lot of people seem to have forgotten. The verb "innovate" is defined as "making changes in something established, especially by introducing new methods, ideas, or products."[2] Many departments and corporate brochures use the term "innovation" to refer simply to things that are "new." But that's only one part of the true definition.

A crucial aspect of the definition is that changes can also be made to something "established." "Innovate" is not a synonym for "create," and its misuse in this way is one of the stumbling blocks to understanding the concept. Innovation, therefore, is also the making of changes in something established by introducing new methods, ideas, or products.

By replacing the word "innovation" with "new" or "new products," it is easier to see how the word is being misused.

Words evolve and take on new meanings and connotations, but it's important to stop and examine precisely what we mean when we say "innovative." Do we just mean "new," or do we have something else in mind? One of the questions I

---

2   *The New Oxford Dictionary*, s.v. "innovate (v.)," accessed September 28, 2022.

ask companies is whether everyone believes they are in the "new" business. Are they in the business of creating something "new" as their primary focus? Is the *next* thing the most important thing? Most companies respond with an emphatic *"no."* The primary focus is on the established now and not on the new future.

"A culture of new products" &
"New products are our primary focus"

CEOs

"We need to be creating new products"

Tech

"This is our most new product"

Sales

"Come work for us...
we are a new products company"

HR

"New efficiencies in the supply chain"

Operations

"We are creating new products"

Marketing

So, what does "innovation" really mean? After years of battling through misuse of the term, I set out to create a contemporary definition of "innovation." This new definition had to encompass both the corporate and startup use of the word. It had to be easy to understand and fit all the corporate use cases above. As I thought about how to define "innovation," I asked myself a simple and, in retrospect, obvious question: "Why do we innovate?" This is an essential question that, for some reason, we gloss over. Why has "innovation" and being "innovative" become so important? The answer I found to "Why do we innovate?" is simply because things change.

Constant change is happening all around us. Nothing stays static for long. With the advent of more and more technologies, the pace of change has sped up. Things change faster now than even a decade ago. Likewise, technology has democratized tools and processes that before were only available to a select few large corporations. This high availability of new tools and processes has further sped up change. Did you know that it is estimated that 100 billion people have ever lived?[3] Currently, we are close to 8 billion people currently living. That means ~8% of anyone who has ever lived is alive right now. That is a lot of people who are effecting change. Soon with the advent of AI, things will further speed up as artificial thought is magnitudes faster than human thought. AI will unlock an almost unlimited number of opportunities to effect change.

With "change" happening at a faster pace and at an increasing scale, we are constantly forced to adapt. Or we can ignore the changes, much like Kodak did with the advent of digital or Blockbuster with the advent of streaming. I think a better word for change would be "evolution." Everything evolves.

3   Ciara Curtin, "Do Living People Outnumber the Dead?" *Scientific American*, September 1, 2007, https://www.scientificamerican.com/ article/do-living-people-outnumber-the-dead/.

The weather, the Earth, the creatures that inhabit the Earth, our thoughts, our desires, our needs, technologies, cultures... everything evolves. Nothing stays static for long. Everything is evolving faster and faster around us. There is also a constant stream of evolution happening within us. It is unstoppable and unavoidable. You can try to ignore the evolutions, but with a guaranteed eventuality, the evolutions will build up and break through all at once. This is when a "disruption" happens. Ignore the evolutions around you for long enough, and you *will* be disrupted. Disruption is not a sudden process. The more evolutionary time that goes by without a response, the bigger the eventual response will need to be to survive.

An example of disruption was when the iPhone launched in 2007. For years before, consumers were wanting to do more and more with the one device that was almost always individually owned: their mobile phone. The team at Apple watched the numerous evolutions that were happening in the mobile phone space—digital personalization with games, wallpapers, and ringtones. Physical personalization where mobile phones were being customized to be as unique as their owners. Service personalization where "apps" on mobile phones were taking the internet everywhere a phone's owner would ever go. Combining the trends above with advances in wireless technology (Wi-Fi, Bluetooth, and cellular) and input advances such as touchscreens, it is easy to see in retrospect all the different evolutions that were combining to create a massive disruption to the companies who were ignoring the evolutions that were happening. Nokia, Blackberry, and Sony-Ericsson come to mind. But not Apple. Apple saw the evolutions that were happening and embraced them.

Most corporate workers are not trained to see the telltale signs of accumulating evolutions that are happening. These telltale signs are also called "trends." If you are observant, you can see the emerging "trends" that evolution is creating. These "trends" have sparse data and sometimes seem almost imaginary, but to a trained innovator, these "trends" reveal the evolution that is happening.

Instead of ignoring the evolutions going on around us, I choose to respond to evolution. Such a simple yet powerful sentence is the previous one: "I choose to respond to evolution." When we "choose to respond" to something, we are acting. We are making a conscious decision to do something to adapt to the new changes evolution is bringing against us.

I believe innovation is that action. Innovation is "the human response to evolution." As the world changes, companies come and go, and consumers, ever fickle, migrate their wants and desires. Evolution is happening; everything is constantly evolving. When we use our minds to respond to the evolutions that are happening, we are innovating. Humans are the only animals capable of creative thought and to be able to take their thoughts and create something new in response to evolution. Animals do not "invent" or "create"; they adapt. Humans, on the other hand, are capable of responding to evolution through invention, using their minds to create something novel to help them respond to evolutions happening around and to them.

So, my technical definition of innovation is:

Innovation is the creation of better products, processes, technologies, or ideas in response to evolution.

I use "better" instead of "new" as I find some of the best innovations a corporation can create are improvements to an existing thing versus always being focused on creating "new" things.

UNDERSTANDING INNOVATION

How companies have been defining innovation is just one way that is a limiter of understanding innovation. Fully grasping the true nature of actually innovating is the next step to being able to implement innovation within your company. The following four traits encapsulate how we use innovation today.

INNOVATION IS CREATED, NOT FOUND

Innovation is not "found." Ideas are not sitting around waiting for someone to "find" them. I am a *creator*. I create things.

I don't sift through an encyclopedia of data in my mind and stumble upon the next idea that excites me—I create ideas by scouring through the data, following the random associations between that data, and inventing something new. Innovation exists just beyond the data in the realm of imagination.

INNOVATION IS CRAZY AND DISRUPTIVE

When I share the idea for any new startup with my friends and family, they usually say it's stupid or crazy or both. In fact, I don't think I've had an idea that people didn't think was crazy at the beginning. Instead of that being a discouraging sign, it's an indication that I'm on the right track. True innovation is fantastic at its inception; it should seem a bit strange and alien. It should feel like a leap in thought rather than a series of incremental predictive steps.

The evolutionary nature of innovation is easy to miss. When people examine the data behind a new, innovative idea, they may imagine a future that is static and unchanging. But when an idea is genuinely innovative, it interferes with projections of the future. In a real sense, true innovation changes the future, and failing to take into account the way that an idea interacts with the future can be a roadblock to understanding the full potential of an idea.

The tendency to disrupt the future is one of the hallmarks of innovation. The word "disruptive" has been thrown around a lot when it comes to discussion about innovation, so it might once again be useful to return to the dictionary. To "disrupt" something is "to interrupt the normal progress or activity of (something)."[4] Notice that the emphasis is on changing something, not creating something completely new. Evolution forces change. How we respond to that change is vital to success.

INNOVATION IS MESSY AND CHAOTIC

The corporate world doesn't like things that are messy because mess implies waste, and operational belief systems try to minimize waste. But innovation, by its very nature, is a messy process full of failed experimentation. Yet those failed experiments go hand in hand with innovation.

Innovation should create a battlefield of failed choices. Analyzing these failed choices eventually allows us to remove the part of the idea that's not valuable. Think of it as creating the perfect diamond. It takes a lot of chiseling and grinding to remove flaws and blemishes, but once you go through the messy process, you're left with a polished, finished diamond that has value. The same thing happens in the process of innovation. Ideas are tried and discarded until all that's left is valuable and effective.

---

4   *The Britannica Dictionary*, s.v. "disrupt (v.)," accessed September 28, 2022, https://www.britannica.com/dictionary/disrupt.

In addition to being messy, innovation can be chaotic, wandering off in unexpected ways. Every time we chisel off some flaw, we might expose something new that we must address. There's no way to plan for innovation because the path is often uncharted. As a process, it's unpredictable. Attempts to put time constraints on it aren't going to be effective. You can't create artificial time constraints on it. I've seen innovations happen rapidly, while others require far more time. The amount of time it can take depends on the individual innovation and the innovators working on it, and progress can't be expected to happen on a neat corporate schedule.

INNOVATION IS RISKY AND DIFFICULT

There are no guarantees in the innovation game. Even new, promising ideas might never end up finding a customer. Some innovations are so disruptive that the time simply isn't right for them to be implemented with success. Likewise, a lot of things that people consider to be new innovations rely on ideas that are becoming obsolete. These innovations may have solved a problem at one time, but they came around too late to be of use in the future.

We live in a world of constant change, of evolution, which makes for a risky environment. It's difficult to operate in such an environment, and anyone that says that innovation is simple or safe is not an innovator. Ultimately, innovation is a creative pursuit, and all creative pursuits involve risk and difficulty. That's not to say that the more difficult an innovation, the more valuable it becomes. It's important not to think of difficulty as a spectrum, with higher rewards for the more difficult innovations. Think of it as a one-setting level: difficult.

INVENTION VERSUS INNOVATION

When I was very sick a few years ago, I watched as doctors spent all my money, trying to find answers. They had no solution or treatment, but they hoped that the answers, once found, would suggest a solution. They were scientifically trained to isolate the problem and find the answers, but they were not trained in innovation or how to create solutions. This is an important concept to understand when it comes to corporate innovation: you cannot "find" innovation; you can only create it.

People often use "invention" and "innovation" interchangeably, but it's important to draw a distinction between the two terms. I see invention as science and innovation as technology. Think of the science classes that you have taken where the goal was to come up with a hypothesis and then test that hypothesis. Through experiment and observation (and hopefully not too many failures), you come up with results that you can then analyze to see if your hypothesis was correct. Ultimately, science is the process of finding answers.

The Difference Between

Invention	Innovation
Focus On Science	**Focus On** Technology
sci·ence | ˈsīəns |noun the intellectual and practical activity encompassing the systematic study of the structure and behavior of the physical and natural world through observation and experiment.	tech·nol·o·gy | tekˈnäləjē |noun the application of scientific knowledge for practical purposes.
Purpose Finding Answers	**Purpose** Creating Solutions
Result(s) Patents	**Result(s)** Products

(& between the two columns)

Innovation, on the other hand, takes the results of science and applies it towards a practical purpose, which is why it is more correctly thought of as technology. Instead of seeking to find answers, innovation focuses on creating solutions. In a corporate environment, we work to find the answers through science and then use innovation to apply those answers in the form of a new product or technology.

As a startup entrepreneur, people often think that I spend my days inventing things. But that's simply a misconception. I'm looking for solutions that involve taking existing science—Wi-Fi or Bluetooth chips, for example—and assembling them in a very specific way in order to create a product that solves a market need. Science finds the answers, but it doesn't reveal the best way to apply those answers. That's where innovation comes in.

We can't find innovation in research reports, market research, trend reports, or consumer focus groups. Sadly, "innovation consulting companies" do not actually help you find real innovation. They can, however, uncover the evolution happening around you and help to see the residual efforts of other people's innovations. These residual efforts leave a set of footprints that a careful innovator can follow in order to map trends and predict likely future developments. By watching the innovations of others and paying close attention to press releases and how products are released, it's possible to project their innovation path out as much as ten years into the future.

A good example of observing trends involves a large beverage company recently testing whether showing videos to consumers before they go to sleep can cause them to dream about their products. This is accomplished by a special kind of video that can trick the brain into remembering things in dreams. Setting aside the ethical aspects of the experiment, this approach has far-reaching ramifications for the future of advertising and innovation. It's not only interesting that the company has decided to go down this path, but it also prompts me to ask why they might be doing the experiment. What do they hope to accomplish? I believe they want to be able to implant their brand not only in the consumer's conscious mind but in their unconscious mind as well. In this example, the science or invention is the ability to plant thoughts into someone's dreams; the innovation is applying the invention to consumer brands through video marketing, helping to create deeper brand awareness.

FOUR CATEGORIES OF INNOVATION

When it comes to innovation, there are four categories to consider:

1. Incremental
2. Radical
3. Revolutionary
4. Theater

These categories are fairly standard and familiar to many people who have studied innovation, but I think about them differently.

Incremental innovation is a series of small improvements or enhancements made to a company's range of products, services, or internal processes. The iPhone is a good example of a truly revolutionary product that reshaped an industry. But when you think about the yearly improvements made to Apple's iPhone since its introduction in 2007, the changes are small: a better camera, longer battery life, and so on. While those small changes were important in driving sales, I don't consider this to be true innovation. It is better described as incremental R&D.

Radical innovation is true innovation. It disrupts the flow of the river. We create something new and move it in a new direction. An example of radical innovation is the launch of Apple's iPhone app store. When they launched the first 2G phone, Apple didn't understand the full value of the device they had created until everybody—and I mean, *everybody*— wanted to create apps for their phone. I was right in the middle of the rush to develop apps, and it was fascinating to watch how many companies were trying to build them. An entire new space was opened. Since the introduction of the app store, there have been countless billion-dollar apps based upon the sensors and other features of the iPhone.

Think about the sensors of the iPhone. There are multiple wireless chips that can connect to any number of devices around us. The invention of the iPhone and its connectivity formed the backbone of many billion-dollar companies. Streaming companies rely on the iPhone's ability to handle large amounts of data quickly and seamlessly. The chips and sensors built into an iPhone—weather sensors, cameras, accelerometers—each is responsible for enabling multiple billion-dollar companies. The app store—that one invention—has probably created more wealth in the world than any other invention in all human history. Yet, when Apple first created the app store, they had no idea just how important their product would be.

Revolutionary innovation is the game changer, the thing that diverts the river in a completely different path. The iPhone itself would fit into this category. In 2007, all the experts predicted the failure of the iPhone, from Steve Ballmer at Microsoft to all the wireless carriers. Everyone thought the iPhone was going to flop because they all believed that a phone with a physical keyboard was the future. Blackberry had become a multi-billion-dollar company by creating a device that dominated the corporate world. It was the de facto standard for a mobile device until the iPhone made it obsolete. The iPhone revolution made the undisputed industry leader irrelevant in a matter of a few years. That's a revolutionary innovation.

Innovation theater is the innovation that is meant to signal to the marketplace that your company is doing future-oriented things. I see this all the time when I go to Consumer Electronic Shows. One example involved a car company that designed a helmet that measured your brain waves so that you could drive with only your brain. Was such a device realistic? No. Could it ever hope to be commercialized in our lifetimes? Probably not. But the concept made that car company's brand seem *innovative*. It was theatrical and memorable, but not much else.

While it's fine to be entertaining and theatrical at times, there are dangers to this "innovation theater." Too often, nefarious individuals use innovation theater to con and manipulate investors and the wider public. A perfect example is Theranos, a company founded by Elizabeth Holmes that claimed to have devised blood tests that required very small amounts of blood and that could be performed rapidly thanks to the small, automated devices the company had supposedly developed. Their claims seemed so revolutionary from the outside, but they never delivered on the promise, which was later proven to be false.

For innovation to be seen as revolutionary or disruptive, it must deliver results. As consumers, we get to decide whether the product is revolutionary or whether it's just a theatrical con.

THE THREE HORIZONS OF INNOVATION

In the corporate world, innovation is often thought of in terms of horizons. The 'Three horizons framework' was initially published by Baghai, Coley, and White (2000).[5] It helps frame innovation when we think about the value created by innovation in the amount of time it takes to create it:

Horizon 1: Operators extend the core. We will talk more about "Operators" in Chapter 3, but the people in charge of managing the operations of the corporation extend the core. This is incremental innovation and line extension. Companies

---

5   Mehrdad Baghai, Steve Coley, and David White, *The Alchemy of Growth: Practical Insight for Building Enduring Enterprises* (New York: Basic Books, 2002).

simply follow the natural progression of something they've already done.

Example: Coca-Cola® adds a new flavor to Coke, an extension of their current line of products. *Coca-Cola Cherry* is an example of an H1 innovation.

Horizon 2: Entrepreneurs develop new opportunities. This usually happens by taking existing inventions and reassembling them into something that has never been seen before and then launching it to the consumer market. Companies have gotten much more efficient in doing this over the last ten years so that the amount of time it takes is approaching the time required for Horizon 1.

Example: Coca-Cola® creates a new drink category, something they have never done before, but which takes advantage of their existing capability. *Coca-Cola® with Coffee* is an example of an H2 innovation where coffee is added to Coke, creating a new type of cola.

Horizon 3: Companies create new inventions that spawn new solutions. This is the time frame where we apply science. Visionaries invent new science that unlocks new solutions.

Example: Coca-Cola® creates an entirely new category. Coca-Cola Creations—along with its first limited-edition product, *Coca-Cola Starlight*—is an example of H3 innovation.

Coca-Cola Creations' goal is to launch new products and experiences across both the physical and digital worlds.

3 Horizons of Innovation

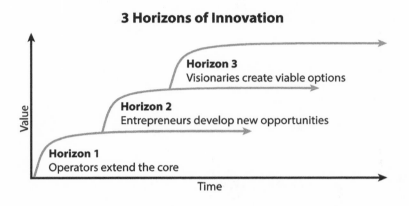

Another way to see the three horizons of innovation is on a graph with market/customer newness on one axis and technological/solution newness on the other. You end up with three broad categories: well-known, new to us, and new to the world.

Just as we have three horizons, we have three personas—corporate managers, innovators/entrepreneurs, and visionaries—and the value that they can create depends on which horizon they are working towards. In the first horizon, for example, visionaries play almost no role at all; in fact, they can dilute the process. Innovators/entrepreneurs can take part in the first horizon process because we can do things more efficiently. Because we are not burdened by the corporate hierarchy, we can launch line extensions more easily.

3 Horizons of Innovation - Advanced

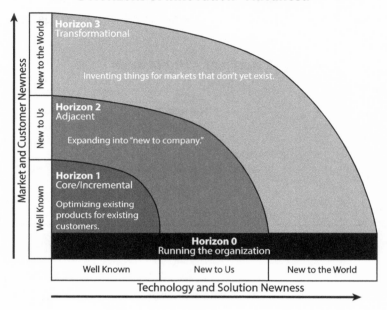

Market and Customer Newness

New to the World

Horizon 3
Transformational

Inventing things for markets that don't yet exist.

New to Us

Horizon 2
Adjacent

Expanding into "new to company."

Well Known

Horizon 1
Core/Incremental

Optimizing existing products for existing customers.

Horizon 0
Running the organization

| Well Known | New to Us | New to the World |

Technology and Solution Newness

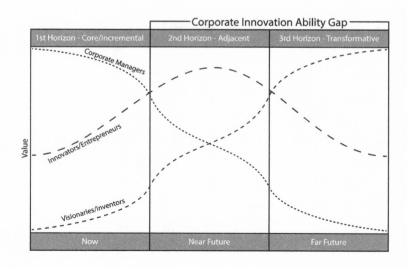

Corporate Innovation Ability Gap

| 1st Horizon - Core/Incremental | 2nd Horizon - Adjacent | 3rd Horizon - Transformative |

Corporate Managers

Value

Innovators/Entrepreneurs

Visionaries/Inventors

| Now | Near Future | Far Future |

Beyond this first horizon, we begin to enter into the corpo-rate innovation gap, the area where corporations struggle at innovation. This "gap" consists of the two horizons where entrepreneurs and visionaries have an entrenched and growing advantage over their corporate competitors.

The second horizon—the adjacent market, the near future—is truly the area of the entrepreneur. Corporate types are on the decline in this horizon, adding less and less value, but visionaries are becoming more important. They're as valu-able as the corporations in this space. There are a lot of fast inventions happening now, and things are moving more quickly from the invention phase into the solutions phase. As a result, the value of visionaries is increasing.

The third horizon, the transformation horizon, is where the visionaries of the world are essential and the corporations have little value. An excellent example of this can be seen with SpaceX, a visionary belief system by someone with a relatively small amount of time in the space industry. On the other hand, NASA would be an example of a big corporate player with a small role now in visionary innovation when it comes to space. If you want to see innovations when it comes to spaceflight today, you'll find it at SpaceX or Blue Origin or some of the other entrepreneurial, visionary ventures.

So much of the corporate world talks about innova-tion in ways that are confusing at best and downright counterproductive at worst. Now that we have a working definition of true innovation, we can work on describing the traits and skills necessary to become an innovator.

CHAPTER 2

WHAT IS AN INNOVATOR?

t was March 19, 2020, when California, where I live, became the first state to issue a stay-at-home order, mandating all residents to stay at home except for essential workers or shopping for essential needs. Within days, I started to get emails from past clients thanking me for helping them create rapid response innovation teams within their organizations. The comments I received all had a similar theme: a lot of innovation had to happen in a small amount of time to be able to stay in business. Even large multinationals suddenly had to take a page from the startups they previously dismissed and begin to think and act more entrepreneurial.

All the corporate rules were thrown out, and the successful companies were able to unleash a small, highly trained
innovation team to rapidly innovate not just to stay in business but to grow during the lockdowns. One head of innovation for a large multinational said to me, "Mike, I finally
understand why you were so adamant that we develop true
entrepreneurial capabilities within our innovation team.
These lockdowns are forcing us to make snap decisions in
high-stress times. I think I finally understand what it is like
to be an entrepreneur."

To best understand the role of an innovator, it's essential to
think about what an innovator is expected to do. If a company
is looking to add an innovative mind to take their business
to the next level, they aren't looking for someone to create
and maintain stability. They're looking to take on a certain
amount of risk in hope of earning a very large reward. They
are looking for special talent.

A company may be full of competent operators—people who
can keep everything operating smoothly and steadily—but
it's wrong to assume that a competent manager can become
an innovator. Innovators are the scientists and engineers
who build the race car, who push the limits of the engine in
order to get as much out of it as they can. But if you put those
engineers in the driver's seat or in the pit crew, they wouldn't
be good at all. They develop the machine for success, but
they don't do well as long-term operators of the machines

they design. I've done a lot of research on what traits are necessary for success when it comes to being an innovator, as well as why those traits are so important.

TRAITS OF AN INNOVATOR

At its core, innovation is 100 percent psychological, and because it is dominated by psychology, it's accessible to nearly anyone. I genuinely believe that anyone can be an innovator, although it obviously comes more naturally for some than others. Innovators are equal parts technologists and artists; they see the world not as it is but as it could be. They spend time in their vision of the future, then come back to the present and build a bridge to that future.

I have always been interested in understanding precisely what traits allow someone to create that vision of the future and then see it through. I have paid close attention to the people I've worked with in both the startup and the corporate realm, hoping to discover the secret to innovation. What I found was a collection of twenty traits that, when present, indicate an enhanced aptitude for innovative thought and action.

Note: In my forthcoming book, *The 20 Traits of Innovators*, I go into the traits in greater depth and also provide online access to an eighty-question assessment.

I have grouped the twenty traits of innovators into five types:

1. **Core Traits**
2. **Self-Feeling Traits**
3. **Self-Thought Traits**
4. **Internal Action Traits**
5. **External Action Traits**

THE CORE TRAITS

- **Fierce**: Innovators show a heartfelt and powerful intensity about their ideas.

- **Inspirational**: Innovators make others want to be a part of and create for their ideas.

- **Hopeful**: Innovators feel optimism about the future of their ideas.

- **Courageous**: Innovators act on their ideas despite danger or disapproval.

The Core Traits of innovators consist of fierceness, inspiration, hope, and courage. These are the four must-have traits for genuinely great innovators. As a startup mentor, these are the traits that I look for when I'm working with founders, and these are the four traits that I try my best to impart to them so that they can develop to their full potential. In the corporate realm, the lack of these traits is one of the primary reasons why corporate innovation teams tend to struggle, which I will address in more detail later in this chapter.

THE SELF-FEELING TRAITS

- **Ambitious**: Innovators always strive for their ideas to reach greater heights.

- **Confident**: Innovators believe in who they are, what their idea is, and their ability to execute their idea.

- **Passionate**: Innovators have intense belief, desire, and enthusiasm for their ideas.

- **Positive**: Innovators shake off failure and bounce back to peak performance quickly.

These are the traits that reflect how people feel internally. Obviously, one's internal feelings towards themselves, their project, and the people that they work with can have a huge impact on their level of success. Do they feel confident? Do they have a passion for the things they hope to create? Do they feel positive? Positivity, especially, is something that I noticed quite a bit following the emergence from COVID. After two years of lockdowns, working from home, and sheltering-in-place, many people finally felt as if they had confronted the greatest challenge of their lives...and survived. In mass, around the globe, people finally woke up to a desire to work on positive things they are passionate about. This newfound "innovator's mindset" has been a leading cause of the "great resignation" that has empowered people to quit their unfulfilling and dispassionate jobs. Moving forward, they want to focus on positive things. Professionally they want to know that they are making the world a better place and not just making their employer more profits.

THE SELF-THOUGHT TRAITS

- **Articulate**: Innovators can readily, clearly, and effectively express their ideas to others.

- **Creative**: Innovators show inventiveness and use of imagination to create original ideas.

- **Curious**: Innovators show a strong desire to know or learn new things.

- **Knowledgeable**: Innovators are polymaths who know a lot about a lot of things.

These traits reflect how someone thinks. Obviously, innovators must think creatively. Perhaps not so obviously, innovators must be extremely curious. Innovation is the process of chasing down and creating a potential future, and if innovators are not curious, they'll never chase down the path that seems too far-fetched to be effective.

Innovators must also be knowledgeable. Note that this is not the same thing as being educated. Some of the worst innovators I've ever met have master's degrees, which can sometimes be a disadvantage because they have learned too much about other people's innovations. Especially in the technology space, innovators need in-depth knowledge about how things are built and usually have a lot of hands-on experience, but getting a degree can be counterproductive in this field because any knowledge gained is likely to be quickly outdated.

THE INTERNAL ACTION TRAITS

- **Diligent**: Innovators work consistently, carefully, and persistently on their ideas.

- **Initiative**: Innovators are the first to take action on their ideas, even if it means acting alone.

- **Resourceful**: Innovators have the ability to find quick and clever ways to enhance their ideas.

- **Versatile**: Innovators are able to adapt to new situations and information quickly.

Internal traits represent the ways that you behave internally and how you bring those internal qualities into the world. Take diligence, for example. Diligence is a vital trait to have when you are facing adversity and hardship. Innovators need to be diligent in the face of failure because failure is something that you will certainly be faced with at some point. Innovators must also show initiative. No one is going to build your idea for you, and it's difficult to hire someone to innovate for you. You must seize the initiative and move the project forward.

Innovators must have the internal initiative to find solutions and be resourceful. In the past, innovators could rely on academia and the corporate environment to provide the resources for solutions. But that is changing quickly, even in heavily academic spaces like biomedical research. Even the most complex technologies are now available to anyone with a credit card. You can order CRISPR gene editing tools delivered to your home or leverage the most advanced AI through a web browser. With the democratization of the tools and technologies used to create new things, internal resourcefulness and curiosity are more important than ever before.

Another internal trait is versatility. Innovators must be comfortable doing all sorts of tasks. Sometimes people get wrapped up in their corporate job title and don't want to venture into other areas, even when it's clearly necessary. They stay within somebody else's preconfigured idea of their role within the innovation process. But in the startup space, creators must be versatile by necessity.

In every startup I've ever created, when we start bringing employees into an office space, I clean the bathrooms. And

I tell every new employee that I, the CEO, clean the bath-rooms. I do this for a variety of reasons. First, it shows them that there isn't a single job at the company that is beneath them. Second, it shows that I care about the members of my team. Another benefit of telling them this is that they are very careful to keep the bathrooms clean when they know the CEO is the one cleaning them. But by far, the biggest ben-efit of cleaning the bathrooms myself is that it conveys pre-cisely how important versatility is in our belief system. In my experience, a team that is versatile finds it much easier to come up with genuinely disruptive innovations.

THE EXTERNAL ACTION TRAITS

- **Coachable**: Innovators accept constructive criticism and incorporate others' ideas into their own.

- **Competitive**: Innovators strive to be the best and beat their competitors.

- **Impactful**: Innovators strive to make their ideas have a substantial effect on the world.

- **Influential**: Innovators can convince others that their ideas matter.

External action traits are simply how we act out in the world. One example of an external trait that is vital for innovators is coachability. If you aren't open to being coached, that means you might not be open to the possibility that you're wrong. I've spent some time working as a coach in the innovation industry, and it's very frustrating to deal with someone who is completely closed off when it comes to taking advice and learning new things.

Innovators must also be competitive, and not just competitive in the way that you might think if you come from a corporate environment. You must be competitive not just against so-called "competitors" but against the entire world. There are so many things in the world that can kill a good idea, and you must have a competitive drive if you want to overcome them. There are going to be things holding you back in your own company, and you must compete against those as well if you want to bring your idea into the world. In fact, more brilliant ideas are killed off within a company than by rival companies. I always find it sad how hard other departments within a large corporation do everything they can to limit innovation within the company. For some reason, these managers would rather the company suffer than let the innovation team succeed. Instead of competing as a team against other companies, they see anyone who may receive credit for a successful innovation as a threat to their own future promotion. What is even sadder is how often large companies totally dismiss any innovation if it is not first developed by them. "Not Invented Here Syndrome" is a very real thing and, unfortunately, infects most large organizations. Every startup founder has a few stories of how they created the next big innovation and were scoffed at by corporate executives when they tried to sell it into the organization. What is fun to watch is when the corporate executives are then told by their own team that they can create the same innovation but better! A year later and hundreds of thousands of dollars down the drain, they realize they should have partnered with the then small startup who is now a year further ahead and stealing their customers. In fact, more brilliant ideas are killed off within a company than by rival companies.

Another external action trait is the need to be impactful. Why work on mediocre ideas that have no impact? True innovation will have an effect on the world, sending ripple effects throughout an industry. Great innovators are always aware of the potential impact of the projects that they take on.

Finally, great innovators need to be influential. Influence isn't just about what you have accomplished in the past, although that is a part of it. When I am brought into a company as an Entrepreneur in Residence, I'm an outsider, yet I'm still able to influence the team, to bring people over to my way of thinking. Being influential in this sense is a skill that you can develop to ensure that others are able to see your idea as valuable and important.

WHAT IS THE MOST IMPORTANT TRAIT?

I get asked frequently what is the most important difference between startup and corporate innovation? My response usually catches people off guard. The number one difference between a startup entrepreneur and an executive in charge of innovations is fierceness. If you are not fierce, you will not be successful. Unfortunately, most companies inadvertently create a culture of fear, and fierce individuals are easily highlighted and cycled out of the business. When everyone is fearful of failure, it's impossible to create the kinds of ideas that will change the world.

It's not irrational for companies to wallow in fear when it comes to the world of innovation. After all, the possibility of failure is a real one. That's why I emphasize fierceness. In fact, if I could only work on one thing upon joining a client company, I'd work on creating a culture of ferocity.

What is fierceness? I define it as embodying a heartfelt and powerful intensity. If innovators don't have that intense spark and approach their project with fierceness, then the innovations they're counting on will never materialize. You must put a part of yourself into a product. If you do, consumers can tell. The public knows instinctively when a product was made by a team that put its heart and soul into the effort and when it was created by a team that was simply checking boxes on a marketing report. A great example of this is the first Apple Macintosh 128K personal computer. Molded inside the case were the signatures of the Macintosh Division employees as of early 1982. They cared so much about their innovation that they went through the additional work to ensure each of their signatures would be forever embossed into the case of each computer sold. Can you imagine a multinational allowing this level of fierce love to be emblazoned on their product today?

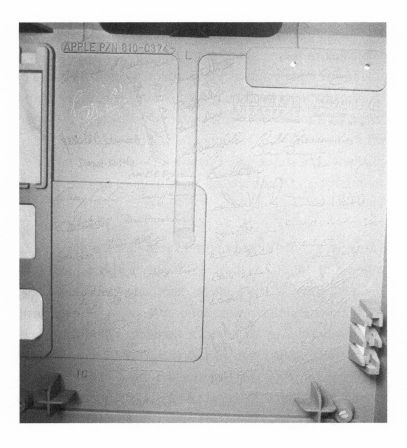

This fierceness that innovators must have to create truly game-changing innovations is now all but extinct in the corporate realm. Yet it is alive and well within the startup world. In fact, it is expected that the fierce entrepreneur places a piece of themselves into the products they create. It is part of the mythos around startup new product creation, and the celebration, by the consumer, of the people who created their favorite new thing.

Fierceness also allows innovative teams to overcome all the obstacles in their path. The amount of competition, both inside a company and out, is substantial, and if you are not personally fierce in all that you do, your idea will never survive. There are just too many ways that a project can be killed off, and it's very easy to simply allow it to happen. Ideas that challenge the status quo will have an even bigger target on their back, and those are the kinds of ideas that innovators look for.

Fierceness is the most important trait, but there are three other important traits that work together with fierceness to make up the core traits of the disruptive innovator. These other traits are inspiration, hope, and courage. In my forthcoming book, *The 20 Traits of Innovators*, I discuss how these traits work together and complement one another. Fierceness amplifies each of the others so that they become *fierce* inspiration, *fierce* hope, and *fierce* courage. Fierceness becomes the critical mindset underlying all innovation.

INSPIRATION, HOPE, AND COURAGE

Inspiration leads to hope, hope leads to courage, courage replaces fear. This saying came to me when I was trying to understand the nature of the magic that happened in the startup world versus the corporate world. Why did innovators seem to behave more effectively when working at a startup? What was the actual recipe for success?

As I went through it in my mind, I realized that the magic always starts with inspiration. And where does inspiration come from? It's not internal. Try to inspire yourself right now. It's impossible. You have to seek inspiration, or it has to be thrust upon you. It's the moment of realization—the "aha" moment. Those kinds of moments don't come out of nowhere.

When inspiration comes, an innovator goes over the idea, thinks it through, and starts creating. Once the idea begins to take shape, hope comes into play. In the corporate environment, they hate the word "hope." I once had someone say to me, "You know, hope is not a strategy." My response to that is, "Hope is the *only* strategy!" Without hope, you will never have any innovation because innovation is a creative process. Your idea does not exist in the world, and it cannot exist until you create it. Hope is what an innovator feels inside—the belief that what we're creating will have value. Without hope, there can be no belief. And without belief, there will only be mediocrity. An innovator without hope won't push against the ceiling of the opportunity, against the competitive forces that want to hold the idea back from its true potential.

Once an innovator feels hope that there is value in a project, they develop courage. Courage comes from hope. Hope is the precursor and is absolutely necessary if you want to have courage. If you think back to times in your life when you managed to do something courageous, you'll find that you felt hopeful. You felt as if you could change the situation. When people are hopeless, when they can't see a way forward, they give up. They won't go against the grain. They won't argue against what leadership wants to do.

The courage created by hope is necessary to overcome the fear inherent in the innovative process. The human brain has a fascinating way to deal with fear. In our brains, the area where we experience courage and fear exist adjacent to one another, and when courage increases, it displaces an equal amount of fear. The inspiration-hope-courage cycle becomes like an engine that creates enough power to push fear out of the way. Combined with fierceness, this cycle allows innovators to succeed and cast aside the many obstacles in their way.

FIERCE INNOVATION

Fierceness and courage are so important because innovation is scary. It's important to remember that innovation is *supposed* to be scary. If it doesn't scare you, then you aren't truly innovating. Innovation exists in risk. This is evident in the startup environment where the comforts and protections of a large multinational corporation are absent, but that scary environment fuels innovation.

The fear of embarking on an innovative journey makes people uncomfortable, but experienced innovators recognize that fear is a necessary part of the process of innovation. Every time I come up with an idea, I know I'm going to go through a scary phase while creating it. And the bigger the idea, the bigger the fear. The more "safe" an idea seems, the more likely it is to be mediocre. It's perfectly fine to feel fear as you are working on a new idea. It's natural and expected. What you shouldn't do is use fear as an excuse to fail to act. It's fine to be afraid, but don't be a coward. Cowards allow fear to control them and become paralyzed by it.

The corporate world tends to reward cowards. Senior executive levels become self-selected for cowardice. Companies, from directors on above, are mostly filled with people who are extraordinarily afraid. Their fear makes sense when you think about their personal and corporate identities. There can be a lot to lose in one's personal life if a corporate idea doesn't work out. They have expensive houses, kids' education, and nice cars to think about, and they crave stability over everything else. Add in the worry about the negative impact on the individuals on their team, and the fear can become overwhelming. As such, they don't value courage because, unlike themselves, courageous people are *willing* to fail a lot.

They fail to understand that courage is the art of failure, not the art of success. Still, when you fail in corporate innovation, there is a bit of protection. The whole business isn't going to collapse. But when you fail in a startup, it's deadly. The company is finished. Startup innovation is much riskier than corporate innovation, but there's something about that risk that unlocks creativity. When we are faced with immense risk, our brains are activated, and we come up with amazing solutions to those risks.

The corporate environment ends up doing precisely the opposite of what they should be doing if they want to build disruptive ideas. But corporations simply don't want to accept that risk is part of the process. They don't understand that the confrontation of risk is actually what leads to the creation of groundbreaking ideas.

If you look closely, you'll notice that consumers are choosing courageous entrepreneurs like Elon Musk over all others. For competent innovators, the risk pays off in the long run.

ARE YOU AN INNOVATOR?

You may look at yourself and think that you don't have what it takes to become an innovator, but that isn't necessarily true. Since innovation is one-hundred percent psychological, it's possible to build the mindset required by developing traits that are associated with great innovators. It won't be easy. It takes great effort to develop and hone those traits, but anything great takes effort. Losing weight requires sweat. There's no escalator on the way to the peak of Mt. Everest. Suffering is required.

What corporations today need to do is treat innovation as an emergency, a special problem that requires a special group of people to solve. Every company needs frontline innovators who can respond to emerging situations with innovative solutions. The experience with the onset of COVID is a good example of what can be accomplished. Some companies didn't respond to the crisis. They hoped the problem would go away on its own. But others flourished because they had sharp, innovative minds who saw the opportunity in the struggle. You don't need me to tell you which kind of firm is better off today.

The frontline innovators are the S.W.A.T. teams of the business world. They are specialized and fierce, ready to launch a plan into action at a moment's notice. They are inspired in the face of chaos, not frightened into paralysis. They leverage their hope into courage and work diligently to build something that will have a positive impact on the world.

Perhaps the best way to understand what an innovator is and what you can do to become one is to define the opposite—the operator.

CHAPTER 3

INNOVATOR VERSUS OPERATOR

When I was a working artist in my youth, owners of professional sports teams would hire me to create artwork for their offices. Sometimes, they'd invite me to sit in their box seats. The games were thrilling, but I also liked to observe people at the games. Owners, athletes, coaches, sports photographers, referees, cheerleaders—even the sports reporters on the sideline—all seemed to be living their dreams. But they didn't make it to where they are by playing it safe. They ended up getting there by taking risks. All those professionals on the field were living their dreams because they believed in taking a risk. The spectators, on the other hand, are satisfied with attending the big sporting event and reveling in the excitement. But they aren't living their dreams the way the athletes that they admire are. The truth is that most people lack the courage to follow their dreams, to truly accept risk in order for a chance at an extraordinary reward. Most people choose to shun risk and are content being a spectator, sitting in the stands of life. Why do some people embrace risk in pursuit of their dreams while others are content to play it safe in the stands?

Within every organization, there are two types of people: Innovators and Operators. Finding the right people and placing them in their proper roles is essential to success, especially when it comes to innovation. Most corporations today are hiring or tasking the wrong people to innovate for them. They are trying to install people who value stability and the status quo into a role that requires risk-taking and rule-breaking. It's vital to fully understand the difference between the roles of Innovator and Operator.

As we discussed in the previous chapter, Innovators are creative entrepreneur types. Operators, on the other hand, are typically MBAs within an organization. They are **M**asters of **B**usiness **A**dministration, and their title describes exactly what they do. They administer or, more specifically, operate the machines that creators create. While the Innovator's primary goal is creation, the Operator is focused on operation and administration. Innovators leverage their experience with and observation of the world around them, whereas Operators tend to fall back on their education and what they've been taught. Innovators create value, while Operators are focused on revenue. Everything within the operation of the business is tied to the revenue of that business. Innovators focus on the future. Operators focus on the present.

Operators love predictability. Operators are the people at a business who make new processes and shape how a company does its business. Traditionally, Operators have been the people in the most senior positions at large corporations. Since the 1970s, operationally trained CEOs have prioritized shareholder value and quarterly tempo above all else. These leaders will come into a business and squeeze out as much profit from existing innovation as possible. CEOs like this are taught to take the beautiful, intricate effort of innovation and wring it out for as much consistent value as possible. Because of this, stability of profit becomes the bedrock of most corporate structures.

Innovators are metamorphic; they are obsessed with radical change, with leaps of advancement. Operators prioritize incremental and predictive growth over radical change. They are frightened by the idea of metamorphosis and rapid change, preferring the comfort and stability of step-by-step growth. Innovators are risk-tolerant. Operators spend the majority of their time thinking about risk mitigation. While

Innovators understand that risk is necessary when pursuing greatness, Operators are uncomfortable with the uncertainty of risk, especially the possibility of failure.

Innovators	vs	Operators
Creative / Entrepreneur		MBA
Creation		Operation / Administration
Experience		Education
Value		Revenue
Focus on Future		Focus on Present
Metamorphosis		Growth
Risk Tolerance		Risk Mitigation

Operators don't make good Innovators, but that doesn't mean that Operators are unnecessary. Both personas are needed for companies to stay relevant and successful. Because innovation is the *human response to evolution*, companies need to have true Innovators to adapt to the evolution occurring around them. New and creative products, processes, technologies, or ideas are the proper response to evolution. We must innovate and change our circumstances in order to adapt successfully. When faced with the need to change, Innovators fall back on their creator skills while Operators fall back on their extensive education. Innovators create knowledge; Operators recite knowledge they have learned.

A good way to expose the difference between Innovators and Operators is how they handle fear. Change can induce fear, and the bigger the change, the greater the fear. Fear is an uncomfortable feeling, but I always know I am innovating when I am feeling afraid. Usually, I feel most afraid when I am working on the riskiest endeavor with a high rate of return. Yes, the fear is uncomfortable, but it comes along with the possibility of great success. For an Operator, the fear can be overwhelming and all-consuming. Even if Operators see the possibilities, the discomfort of possible failure prevents them from responding to evolution and embracing and celebrating risk. They are unwilling to be uncomfortable in the face of fear, and that's a problem. The mitigation of fear becomes the ultimate goal. Fear is uncertainty, and reducing the severity, seriousness, or painfulness of fear becomes their priority. Innovators see risk as an additive process, making their ideas bigger in the face of risk. Operators see risk as a subtractive process, making their ideas smaller to lessen the risk. In corporate meetings, I can always tell the Innovators and Operators in the room. When talking about a new innovation, Innovators naturally want to make the idea bigger, even if it means increasing the risk. They view risk as the thing that actually makes the idea something special—a kind of talisman, revealing that they are on the right track. The Operators in the meeting want to discuss how to "risk mitigate" the idea down in size. They want to cut a bit here and trim a bit there, shrinking the idea down to make the risk more tolerable. To them, the risk is something to "mitigate," not something to celebrate. Have you ever noticed how much smaller an innovation becomes after it makes the rounds through the departmental approvals process? This shrinkage happens when risk-prone Operators conform an innovation to their own personal tolerance of risk. Trimming an idea down to make it "comfortable" risk-wise is a sure sign your company is failing at innovation.

I like to think of Innovators as the people who build race cars. They are the individuals who understand the science and technology and who have the ability to turn that technology into something beautiful. A race car is a stunning piece of technology. Being around an engineer who can create an amazing machine from scratch is the same as being around a great artist. They are like da Vinci, blending the expertise of the technician with the creativity of the artist. A talented engineer/innovator speaks with an artistic lexicon, even if it includes a lot of technological jargon. For example, they might listen to the hum of the engine and talk about it in musical terms. They see innate beauty in their creations. To them, their creations by themselves are works of art—much like a Stradivarius violin, which is a beautiful creation all on its own, yet it becomes something even greater when a skilled operator begins to play it.

The pit crews and the race car drivers are the Operators. They take the innovation and do something with it. If you try to picture a racing team without seasoned drivers and a competent pit crew, you will understand that the role of Operators is just as valuable. You can't be a winning race team or a successful corporation without Innovators and Operators. Drivers understand how to turn that machine into something beyond what it seems to be, a tool to perform with. The same thing is true of pit crews. They understand innovation in graphic detail. Although they didn't create it, they can make it sing. They have their own level of artistry to add.

Companies need both Innovators and Operators, and they need them in a certain ratio. You need more people operating a machine than you need people who are inventing a machine. For example, the internet is arguably one of the greatest inventions of our time. But it was a small group of people who came up with the protocols, the software, and the hardware to make the internet happen. Now, billions of people are operating on top of that invention.—a small group of Innovators, and a much larger group of Operators.

Another example of the Innovator/Operator model can be found in the science-fiction series *For All Mankind*, an alternate history depicting what would have happened if we had never stopped going to the moon. When I watched the show, I recognized that the engineers—the creators of the technology—were the Innovators in that scenario. They were responsible for the massive innovations necessary to explore space. The space suits, engines, rockets, capsules— even the dehydrated food—were all the result of engineer Innovators pushing the limits of technology.

Mission control played the role of Operators. Everyone on the team is well-versed in science, all of them trained, almost certainly with degrees from the best technical universities. Their training and experience gives them the know-how to run the day-to-day operations of that mission. The technology created by the engineers requires them to be very good at what they do.

As I continued watching I realized that there is another persona in this scenario. Some people would say that the astronauts are the Operators, but I see them fulfilling another role. The astronauts are the entrepreneurs, the ones stepping into a high-risk and extremely dangerous environment, leveraging the impressive innovations to unlock even more knowledge. Mission control gets to go home at night. They eat three meals a day on a consistent schedule. Sure, they have to deal with stressful and unplanned situations, but those are nothing compared to what the astronauts face tens of thousands of miles from the Earth.

This analogy illustrates how a big government organization like NASA operates in a fascinating way that can be emulated in the corporate environment. Most corporations already have the equivalent of Mission Control in place. They also have a group of engineers who are tasked with the creation of new incremental innovation. What is missing is the "astronauts," the people who are comfortable with risk and encouraged to think beyond the company's incremental innovations—the risk-takers who are tasked with responding to the disruptive evolutions that will potentially destroy the company.

Companies need a group of people willing to take high risks, to take on their innovations, and see the market as a high-risk environment. In most corporations, our incremental-innovators are asked to do that, but they are being asked to be half-operator, half-innovator. Successful companies understand that such mixed roles are psychologically impossible for one person to fill. Most engineers don't want to work on the business side of an idea; they don't feel comfortable as Operators. They don't want to bring the solution to market. Their sole goal is to develop an idea and create solutions. At the same time, mission control—the Operators of the business—don't want to innovate. Not only do they not want the responsibility of creating new things, they want to keep new things to a minimum. They have already achieved operational excellence on the technology they have at the moment. Future innovations will require them to rework a system that, from their vantage point, is already optimized.

In most companies, there is a large gap in the number of high-risk individuals and high-tolerance individuals who want to advance the solution into the marketplace. There is one mission, but it requires three different sets of skills. Finding the proper ratio between those skill sets is the blueprint that will allow companies to be more successful when it comes to innovation.

ILLUSORY SUPERIORITY

Executives tend to suffer from a cognitive bias called "illusory superiority." This affliction occurs when a person believes that they "are better than average in any particular metric."[6] In other words, those who hold an MBA—which includes most executives—overestimate the value that an MBA brings to contemporary leadership. They think that because they have an MBA, then other people who have an MBA are better at solving innovations because their shared education is "better" than someone without an MBA.

Since most executives are trained MBAs themselves, they tend to place a high value on their qualities associated with advanced business degrees. Who better to create a new product than someone like myself? *they think. As a result, they assign innovation-oriented projects to people with similar experience to themselves. The problem with this approach is that the world has radically changed in the past ten years. When executives came up through the ranks, having an MBA* and *creating new products worked well together. They had more time to figure things out, and an MBA could get both jobs done. But recently, a radical shift has taken place. Never in the history of the world has it been*

---

6   Scicurious, "The Superiority Illusion: Where Everyone Is Above Average," *The Scicurious Brain* (blog), Scientific American, April 1, 2013, https://blogs.scientificamerican.com/scicurious-brain/the-superiority-illusion-where-everyone-is-above-average/.

easier to create a new product or start a new company. Once only available to corporations, the tools of innovation are now democratized and available to everyone.

For example, consider the beverage space. Most of the new products launching and gaining consumer interest come from startups. Launching a new beverage was once a costly, time-consuming ordeal, perfectly suited for the MBA skill set. Today it takes only a few dedicated people to move a product from concept to retail shelf in a fraction of the time and cost that it took ten years ago. Add to that the proliferation of freely available marketing tools, and it's clear that it has never taken so little to go big.

CEOs are usually the people who are tasked with the initial response to disruption within their industries. A response almost always comes from the top down. But when you look at the details, you'll notice that most CEOs were trained in operational excellence, since their day-to-day business is dominated by operational concerns. They have very little experience when it comes to innovation. The market doesn't give a premium on innovation excellence, so those skills are de-emphasized. Cost cutting and other operational responses, on the other hand, will move the market. CEOs are incentivized to concentrate on operational excellence, which then causes them to feel an illusory superiority.

The dominance of operational thinkers in corporations misleads them into hiring the wrong people to innovate. True Innovators seem weird to the Operators of the corporate world. I've been called weird many times. That's fine. I am weird. I'm not like them; I am not an Operator. I don't think operationally about problems; I think about innovative solutions to problems. I don't look at the existing list of solutions; I create new solutions. Focusing on new solutions is a far more effective way of solving a problem. Rehashing old solutions is no way to face the future, and I look to the future. MBAs look to the past.

When you think about the operation of the machine, you want backward-facing data. Operational minds love data because they are good at going through and finding the operational efficiencies that the data exposes. I've been in many meetings where a problem was highlighted with stacks of spreadsheets. I tell them that the data they want to show me is irrelevant. We're creating the future. There is no data yet, so there can be no spreadsheets to contain it. There's only a plan, an instruction book to create our own data as we innovate. Innovation is the process of creating first-party data. We can't rely on research reports or trend reports or any external data sources. We need to create first-person data that will give us more truth about a project than anything filtered through other people. When people pull in a third-party, they are operating.

Most executives think they are super smart—and they are...until they find themselves in my world. When one person in the room challenges your "illusory superiority," it breaks the illusion and *suddenly you can have a truthful conversation. One of the nice things about having someone in the executive team who is external but attached, like an Entrepreneur in Residence, is the ability to challenge the Executive Leadership team without consequence. I usually have the freedom to question assumptions and the ability to see a problem from an entirely new angle. It is one of the primary reasons I get hired, usually by the CEO. To get executives to begin to think and act more entrepreneurially. To help them see innovation not as something filled with risk but to see it as a tool to unlock consistent future growth.*

The goal should be to establish a business model set for innovation that is separate from the operational excellence side of the business. There are two cultures, and it's counter-productive to push away great Innovators because they seem "weird" or different.

ARE YOU AN INNOVATOR OR AN OPERATOR?

If you consider our education system from pre-kindergarten all the way through to an advanced degree, and examine the curriculum employed, you'll find that most of the degree programs offered end up creating Operators. There is not a lot in our current education process that develops and nourishes Innovators. For example, I was never offered a class on risk tolerance.

When I was at college, the dean of the school came and talked to me. She said that I had more college credits than anyone who was currently enrolled there. I had more than a PhD level of education. When I reflect on all that learning, I realize that there isn't much that I use on a day-to-day basis. More than my education, it was my art career that taught me how to be a great innovator and a successful entrepreneur. The creation process for artists is very similar to the technology creation process.

When I first meet people, I like to ask them whether they are Innovators or Operators. And when I do, most people describe operational excellence and the rewards that they can get from being a great operator versus innovation excellence. Well over 90 percent of the time people describe themselves as Operators instead of Innovators.

I like to remind them that we were all Innovators once, before the education process got a hold of us. When I would interact with my nieces and nephews, before the school process got a hold of their little brains, they were brilliant Innovators. They had wild imaginations and zero qualms about the creative process. I could give them a marker and say, go draw X. And they would draw X, no matter what it was. I could imagine the craziest stuff, and they would try to draw it. They had no fear at all when it came to being creative. If I inspired them, they found hope and courage and went through the process that all great Innovators go through. On top of that, they had no anxiety about showing their creations to me. They were not self-conscious. They had no problem interacting. Even my shy nephew was immensely capable. Once he had broken through the shyness and settled down, he became immensely innovative.

We then kill off that creativity through education. Our educational process does nothing to promote excellence in innovation. We teach children that operational excellence is the only kind of excellence that exists. We take creative kids and we kill off the Innovators inside them to make sure that they can fit in at the future office they are being educated for. We train people to be great at operating machines, and make no mistake, a computer in an office is a machine. Almost our entire education system focuses on operations and neglects the skills needed for innovation. That's a shame, because the world needs brilliant people to solve wicked problems by envisioning a future with the courage to build it. Without Innovators we will try—and fail—to operate against evolution with increasingly out-dated machines.

RESPONDING TO EVOLUTION

There is a deep human need to create. Long ago, when there was very little technology, farming and crafts were creative pursuits. When you think of pre-industrial skills, you think of things that have far more to do with innovation than operation. A preference for innovation is built into human evolution. This failure to nurture innovation may be one of the causes of the Great Resignation unfolding in 2022. COVID presented an existential threat, and people simply reacted to it on a personal level. Facing the possibility of death can put things into a different perspective. People tend to go over their lives, and evaluate past decisions. They think back to when they were young and how much fun they had creating. When I talk to people pursuing a career change, many times their primary reason for wanting a change is that they are seeking fulfillment. They need to satisfy something innate inside themselves. The vast majority of human beings are not fulfilled by operational excellence alone. My guess is that if you are an "Operator" at work, you have external hobbies or interests that fulfill your inner "innovator." Being a competent widget-maker or moving data from one pile to another is not fulfilling in and of itself. Operating a machine, even if you operate it

immensely efficiently, doesn't fulfill you the way creating
something from scratch will.

From an evolutionary perspective, we still need creative
solutions to the problems we face. The operational solutions,
by themselves, no longer work in a fast-paced environment.
Corporations are finally waking up to the fact that there
needs to be a new emphasis on creativity. Unfortunately,
they are totally unprepared to be able to increase the scale
of their innovation because they have the wrong idea about
who the most effective people are. They don't have the right
framework and the right belief system within their organizations to respond to evolution because they rely on people
who received an outdated education, which is too operationally focused. They need instead to tap into the innate five-
year-old, the creative spark that has been suppressed for so
long. That's where they'll get the answers to create the future.

Evolution is happening. The only way to respond to evolution
is by creating the future that responds to it. That is all innovation really is. It's a creative pursuit, so we should be running
our big businesses as creative pursuits, not as operational
pursuits. Operational efficiencies don't mean much if you
can't respond to the sweeping changes that are constantly
occurring. You can't operate yourself out of irrelevance. The
big companies who have tried have found themselves disrupted by a younger, better version of the future, a future
that the company could have owned if it had invested more

energy in innovation. Instead, there's a tendency to allow the MBAs who know only about operations to dominate the creative process. This approach makes no sense. It's like asking a race car driver to design a new piston system. Success just isn't possible.

I have seen it happen again and again. Companies neglect innovation, and they aren't ready for the big changes that inevitably arrive. If you are in executive leadership, you need to change how you think about the operations of your business. You need to instill more creativity and emotion into your business. You need to celebrate both operational excellence *and* innovative excellence. You need to acknowledge that you run the business with an emphasis on operational excellence to appease your shareholders, through cost-cutting, a focus on revenue, and increased profits. But that operational excellence is temporary. All of it is irrelevant if you can't create the next "something"—and the next thing is always a creative pursuit. You need to create a *new* culture within your business so that Innovators have the opportunity to be exceptional. It's not a scaling problem or a talent problem. It's a psychological problem, and the good news is that it's easy to fix if you have the courage to do it.

For every single person who is celebrated by society—actors, musicians, authors, sports stars, and influencers—there was a point where they created something and put it out there for others to evaluate. We reward that with attention, encouragement, and our dollars. If they take a big enough risk and they have enough talent, then they rise. Celebrating talented risk-takers is essential to the human experience. That is how the innovation process works. Established corporations must understand that having professional risk-takers within an organization will create value that an audience can celebrate, hopefully with their money. If they don't, then they might lose their audience to a forward-thinking, risk-tolerant company, most likely a startup.

CHAPTER 4

STARTUPS
VERSUS
CORPORATES

n less than 24 hours, Elon Musk shipped out Starlink, a satellite internet constellation operated by his company SpaceX and unlocked internet access to the government and the people of Ukraine during the first few days of the 2022 Russian invasion. This is a feat that only an innovator could accomplish. No one asked or expected giant corporations like AT&T, Comcast, or Globalstar to step in and provide immediate internet access under such conditions. Instead, they asked the most famous contemporary innovator, and he delivered.

It's a pattern that keeps repeating. Huge multinational companies get caught flat-footed and lose market share to innovative startups. But why is this happening? Why do corporations fail to execute billion-dollar ideas, despite having time, talent, and treasure in abundance? This is the trillion-dollar question.

Over the last thirty years, the corporate environment has shifted, allowing startups to gain a foothold in previously inaccessible spaces. The most obvious change could be described as the democratization of the tools of innovation. Startups began leveling the playing field when open source software became mainstream. In the past, the tool set that an innovator needed wasn't readily available to startups, often because it was prohibitively expensive. Today, there is no secret knowledge or special tool that isn't either free or available for an affordable monthly fee.

The democratization of innovation has revealed advantages of structure and mindset that have allowed startups to gain market share at a shocking pace. In the current environment, startups have become optimized to confront evolution with innovative solutions, while their bigger, slower counterparts worry about risks that evolution uncovers. The constant evolution of the world gives these streamlined startups an abundance of opportunities to make an impact on the future.

WHY DO STARTUPS INNOVATE
BETTER THAN CORPORATIONS?

In a corporate environment, any mistakes innovating can be blamed on the company itself and not the individual(s) who created them. They become mere employees, one of thousands, making them abstracted from the company. On the other hand, entrepreneurs are judged *personally*. Their creations become tightly associated with their public and private image. When the decision is completely on you, it unlocks something in the human experience.

AUDACIOUS IDEAS

"Audacious" is the perfect word to describe how startups innovate *and* operate. It simply means "showing a willingness to take surprisingly bold risks."[7] That attitude is one of the clearest distinctions between startups and corporates. Startups base their entire existence around an audacious idea, and they build audacious innovations on an audacious timescale. They gain an advantage by responding more quickly to evolution. Corporations tend to wait for third-party confirmation of the changes that they see in the market, and they often get beaten to the punch.

---

7   *New Oxford American Dictionary*, s.v. "audacious (adj.)," accessed
      September 28, 2022.

Waiting is not an effective strategy for dealing with evolution. The corporate culture wants to wait till a problem fully develops and then find a solution. But there are innovators around the world who understand that true innovation isn't found; it's created. They seek out the opportunities revealed by the changing environment, and they work early on to create solutions. Climate change is a great example of this phenomenon. There's one group of individuals who advocate waiting to respond to the threat until it comes into absolute focus, either for selfish reasons or because they like the status quo. But the creative individuals—the true innovators— are creating technologies now, in advance of the threats and ramifications, that have the potential to save a large number of lives. The willingness to take on great risk in order to effect a great impact is a key characteristic of startup psychology.

People in startups pay close attention to the incremental progression of evolution and anticipate what's going to evolve next. When the changes happen as they predict, they create solutions that dazzle people, because it seems almost like magic. When changes happen that they did not predict, they quickly pivot, or as I like to say "tack," to new solutions based on the unfolding evolution. ("Tack" or "tacking" is a sailing term that means "to change course by turning a boat's head into the wind." I like "tack" instead of "pivot" because pivoting implies stopping whereas "tacking" is all about finding the wind of opportunity to maintain forward progress.) Commercializing things at just the right time is crucially important for innovators, and the slow-moving corporate environment doesn't stand a chance.

Startup innovators are drawn to big changes while corporate innovators strive for incremental change. Even if someone in the corporate world has an audacious idea, by the time it goes through the approval process of an executive leadership team, it's been whittled down to half its original size...at least, if not killed entirely. Companies never approve innovations as they were created by innovators. They find the ideas too audacious, too risky.

Companies are often all too happy to settle for "enough." The fear of failure prevents them from responding with large leaps of innovation and, as a result, they get leapfrogged by their startup competitors. The focus on doing "enough" to respond to the evolution of the world isn't effective because evolution never stops. By the time you build something that is just "enough," you need something else. Responding to every small change in this incremental way is highly inefficient. To make gains, you must anticipate the future and build for it.

Often these corporate executives can imagine that future, but they don't trust that their team can build that future. Executives should trust their innovators more than they trust themselves, because the innovators have more courage and a higher tolerance for risk. Executives need to recognize that they are operators. If they've assembled a team of *true* innovators who have the twenty traits of innovation, then they must learn to trust that their team is going to do their job and create an amazing innovation for them to operate.

I go into much more detail on who innovators are and how to identify them and put them to work on a team in a forthcoming book, *Disruptive Innovation!—How Corporate Innovators Can Quickly Create Mass Disruption*, coming out in 2023.

WILLINGNESS TO RISK

For the past twenty years, startups have dominated the corporate space with no sign of stopping. They have done so by being nimble, dexterous, and able to shift to any change in the market. Yet very few large companies have responded in a meaningful way to the success of startups. Corporate innovators a decade ago relied heavily on third parties for their data and everything was pre-planned. The innovators of ten years ago were masters of stability and consistency.

Those same standards of excellence in the 2010s are handicaps now.

The contemporary innovator is fluid, flexible, and able to adapt to whatever is thrown at them. They respond to evolving markets and problems with mobility and a willingness to blow up whatever isn't working. Using democratized technology, contemporary innovators respond to seismic developments with whatever tool—from whatever discipline—as needed. In brief, innovators today have the entrepreneur-mindset.

Again and again, the finest chief innovation officers come from acquisitions. A traditional company will acquire a promising startup and bring the founder into their leadership team. These entrepreneurs cut their teeth on innovation by building a business out of scratch. Startup founders have experienced what it's like to strike out on their own, identify a market, launch a product, get it to a consumer, and grow it. After going through all that, they cannot see the world any other way. Entrepreneurs see their world in terms of innovation, in what can be improved, in what can be pared away. These are the people who are best suited to head up innovation at any company.

In the year 2022, the overwhelming majority of businesses and their innovation efforts are run by innovation-averse operators who were taught through their MBAs to do everything the exact opposite way. This is why contemporary companies are losing the arms race with startups: they are founded on and led by a fear of innovation.

Why are so many people afraid of innovation, even if they don't realize it? Because innovation is risky. And risk is scary, especially to operators and the shareholders that I report to.

There is nothing inherently wrong with avoiding risk, but the new paradigm of the business world—empowered by easily accessible technology and rapidly changing markets and consumer bases—favors a bolder, riskier approach. In a more rigid world, a rigid mindset is more appropriate. Our world now is far from rigid; if anything, it's too fluid and dynamic.

The tangible difference between a startup and a traditional company is that a startup embraces risk, and a company pushes it away. Just look at investment.

Silicon Valley has been flush with capital for going on twenty years. Tech startups are practically guaranteed investment at inception. Still, for every tech startup founded, as many fail or get subsumed into a larger entity. Startups are a highly volatile space where risk is baked into the foundation of the product. Instead of deterring investors, however, this risk draws in funders.

Investors have figured out what traditionally run companies haven't; in the contemporary economy, enough risky bets will pay off such that innovation and genuine ingenuity trump stability.

At the same time that startups are swimming in investments, traditional companies are begging for funding. The money is out there, but most corporations haven't figured out how to draw it in. By rejecting risk, these businesses reject innovation; by rejecting innovation, they scare off investors.

BIG WINS VERSUS SMALL SAVES

Most startups focus on the big win, while most corporates focus on the small save. The corporate view is negative, while entrepreneurs view things more positively. Much of corporate strategy involves protecting what they already have. This is the exact opposite of entrepreneurs, who think mostly about gaining, or more accurately *creating*, something new. Startups have an offensive, positive strategy that is simply better suited to the goals of innovation. Being offensive minded—looking for the big win—is one reason why startups are outperforming their corporate competitors.

Companies are simply bad at making decisions when it comes to innovation. There are usually far too many people involved in the process. Many times the decision-makers don't want to be embarrassed by a possible failure. Their attitude turns defensive. They delay responding to evolution because they think solutions will present themselves. And the solutions will reveal themselves when their competitor takes the advantage of being the first mover, and they will then get to experience their competitors' solutions and not their own. Even then they can only delay innovating until the changes become so great that they are forced to take an action, thinking that the crisis will insulate them from criticism. Unlike true innovators, they play it safe even as they are losing.

Interestingly, a lot of startup entrepreneurs have the same level of risk tolerance in their personal lives as they do in the business world. For instance, there are a lot of startup entrepreneurs who compete in extreme sports. You see more startup founders running marathons in the desert than corporate executives because they tend to look for large challenges. I would know; I have been an ultrarunner for a longtime. Startup entrepreneurs like me think exponentially rather than incrementally. When I'm recruiting people, it's always a good sign when their interests outside of work align with an exponential, innovator's mentality.

Because they are used to risk, entrepreneurs become used to failure. They aren't embarrassed by it, so it can't frighten them into inaction. Corporations would be wise to search out people who embrace failure, who aren't scared to talk about their failures and what they've learned from them. Of course, you want them to have enough successes to be able to understand what success looks like. One thing I always tell people about myself is that I have built all kinds of companies. Most of them failed, but that's okay. I've learned more from my failures than from my successes. I'm just blessed that the weight of my successes are greater than the weight of my failures. Out of the twenty-two companies I created when I was a startup entrepreneur, only ten were successful. That's a lot of failures. Yet when I've succeeded, my success was huge. That's why innovators are focused so much on the big win.

DIRECT CONNECTION TO CUSTOMERS

Startups have an advantage over corporations when it comes to making connections with customers. Since entrepreneurs are involved in every aspect of their startup, they tend to have more direct contact with customers. This direct contact can pay dividends in multiple ways during the innovation process.

On the other hand, companies do care what their customers think. In fact, many companies spend large amounts of money on research that tells them what their customers think. Then they use that research to build products that they *think* their customers want. They believe the research, and why wouldn't they? They likely paid quite a bit of money to hire a large consulting firm to collect it for them.

Part of the problem is that people lie to focus groups. I have watched countless corporate innovation focus groups, and the participants almost always talk about what they know— their past and their present. Yet innovation is the art of creating the future, and the average consumer focus group participant is not trained to imagine the future, so they provide limited, pedestrian insights. Combined with the inability of large consulting firms to source original, first-party data, the "insights" they sell are lacking. Here is a dirty little secret of the "reports" sold by large consulting firms: they interview entrepreneurs like myself about the current evolutions and the solutions we are creating and turn around and sell these "insights" for a premium to corporate clients. Big companies should be creating their own first-party data. I never trust the third-party data because 1) it is usually outdated and 2) it is resold again and again to all other large competitors, rendering the data unvaluable for innovative pursuits.

Big companies shouldn't trust anyone else to create or gather innovation-specific data for them. They should conduct their own observations in order to find out their customers' true preferences. Form a relationship internally with your consumers, and let them participate in the co-creation of your innovations. If you have anybody between your innovators and your customers, you're going to fail.

Startups already work directly with their customers. Even the founder of the startup will interact personally with the customer. This interaction allows them to collect valuable first-party data, even if it is sometimes anecdotal. And when consumers can interface with a company at its early stages, they tend to share more information because they realize and appreciate the fact that they have a hand in the creation of the product. This kind of interaction unlocks the inner innovator in the *customer*. They get to go on the building journey with the company. The minute a company hires someone from the outside to interact with their customer, that connection is severed. The product becomes inauthentic. It feels like a corporate product, and the customer becomes indifferent to it. I have seen this happen again and again, usually with large consulting firms. They collect data from your consumer, on your behalf, and then filter it so it meets what *you* asked them to originally collect. They do not want to disappoint you and potentially lose you as a customer, so they stay within the guardrails of what you asked them to find. However, evolution is unpredictable and will zig and zag. Most of the time it will cross over the guardrails of what you originally thought and take off into a new and unpredicted direction. When this happens, if you are not in control of the research, you will not discover this new direction. Your intermediary will not follow the early telltale signs, hoping to maintain the original client vision, for fear of losing their contract.

In a startup there is usually a single vision for the product that is informed by a direct observation of the customer's response to it. The end product is directly connected to what the customer desires, and any changes are based on high-quality first-person data. In most large companies, on the other hand, designs are based on unreliable third-party data and then sent on to department after department, each adding its own interpretation of the vision. The end product becomes muddled. For example, I hate using Microsoft Word because it has too many features. It feels bloated and unwieldy. This happens because there are too many people involved in the innovation of that product, and everyone wants to add something with little regard for how well it fits into the project as a whole.

Here is a fun image I share with my clients to illustrate this point:

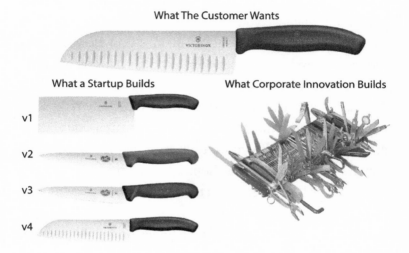

What The Customer Wants

What a Startup Builds   **What Corporate Innovation Builds**

v1

v2

v3

v4

ARTIFICIAL LIMITS

Corporate innovators are often self-conscious about violating the norms associated with their industry. A great contemporary example of this is beverage companies refusing to explore the opportunities created by the legalization of cannabis in many states. They tell themselves that they only sell alcohol in their business. Or they convince themselves that the customer will never switch to a different intoxicant.

They search for excuses *not* to take action. But most of their excuses are simply personal belief limits that they impose on themselves.

These self-imposed limits are based upon bad psychology, negative emotions, and poor logic. Often, they are imposed because the people involved don't want to be embarrassed. Sometimes people tell me that they can't pursue a project because they "don't want to damage the brand." When I ask more specifically how the brand would be damaged and what the ramifications of that damage would be, they don't have good answers. It's clear that fear of embarrassment and damaging their *personal* brand is driving how they think about the project.

And since corporations love to try and innovate with a couple dozen people in the room, there are a lot of personal fears to sort through before you can find a path forward. Everything must be discussed, and every person must have his or her say. There's too much talking. Too many plans are made, and precious few actions are taken. Planning too much keeps your true innovators tied up on video calls and watching PowerPoints when they should be in the business of taking action and creating the innovation.

Becoming so devoted to planning is too limiting. Take personal vacation planning, for example. It's possible to over-plan a vacation, to do too much research and have a

completely full itinerary. Those kinds of vacations are usually not the most memorable. Rushing from one planned
activity to another, even if you're having fun in the moment,
you have to stop and move on to the next agenda item. The
best vacations I've had were not well researched at all. I pack
my shorts, some flip-flops, and my passport and head out
the door for a grand adventure. These vacations where I pick
a destination and let my decision-making happen in the
moment always turn out to be the best. If you look back at
your life, you'll find that sometimes the most unplanned and
unscripted things were actually the most enjoyable because
you become wrapped up in the mystery of the experience.

It's difficult to pre-plan art, and innovation is much closer
to art than the corporate world would like to admit. In my
art career I often did little preparation—a simple sketch to
inspire the owner of a building I wanted to paint a mural on,
and then I would pour everything I had into the final version.
When it comes to my startups, I didn't plan much on the successful ones. The ones that were the most successful were
the ones that only had a simple vision at the start; the rest of
building it was based on "in the moment" decisions. The ones
that failed sometimes failed because of too much planning.
I tried to guess too much about what the future was going
to be like instead of *actually* creating the future. In a startup,
innovators are freer to respond to evolution because they
can change the plan as needed, at any time, without needing
to first get approval from seven committees.

FACTS VERSUS EMOTION

Startups can often raise more capital, for a specific inno-vative idea, than a large corporation can. Part of this goes to their focus on the big win, which draws investors. But another factor is that startups are usually excellent at tell-ing a great story and creating an emotional connection with investors (and consumers as well). The corporate presen-tations on innovation tend to show slide after slide of over-flowing data and facts. Facts don't get funding. Great stories get funding. Facts just support the reason to fund.

When you look at presentations created by startups, you'll find that they operate on very few facts. That may sound like a deficiency, but facts are usually created and documented through research. If the research is already available from another source, then there's a likelihood that the research is outdated or a competitor has already taken this research and is executing on it. As an innovator, I want to create my own facts by collecting my own first-party research. The last thing that any innovator wants to do is rely on facts that have been made obsolete by the evolution that has taken place since they were first collected.

Instead of a long list of facts, an entrepreneur gains inter-est by presenting a story centered on a great vision. A tal-ented presenter can engage an audience on an emotional level, because great innovators feel strong emotions about their ideas. The emotional angle is lacking in most corporate presentations, which rely solely on convincing an audience on a logical level, with slide decks overflowing with data. The impact is much greater when emotions are involved. When people fall in love, they don't do it on a logical level. Innovators have the ability to get people to fall in love with their idea. They are able to get their audience to feel the same kind of hope and excitement that they feel. When they have an emotionally impactful story to go along with their idea, it can override any logical arguments that corporate types think are the ultimate means of persuasion.

Of course, it's possible that the emotional aspects of a founder's story conceal the reality that the idea just isn't very good. There are many stories that rely on false emotion, and they are used to generate interest in false innovations. There's a balance between the emotional and the logical appeals when it comes to innovation. The vision of an idea has to make sense emotionally, but the logic has to be there as well. The problem for corporations is that they don't understand the emotional aspect of innovation, and, in fact, they ridicule the very idea of emotion being involved at all.

Emotion creates passion, which can help drive a difficult but worthwhile idea to completion. Since entrepreneurs have more of themselves wrapped up in their innovations, they tend to be more passionate. They think about their innovations and what needs to be done all the time. I can email my startup friends at 5:00 pm on Friday, and they will respond almost immediately. Probably no one in the corporate world will respond at 5:00 pm on a Friday. In a corporate environment, people tend to wash their hands of "work" at the end of the day or week. They either don't have the emotional commitment to "work" in their off time, or they assume that someone else on the team will take care of it for them.

HOW I PRESENT

As an EIR (Entrepreneur in Residence), when I present an idea to a client company, my slides are radically different from my corporate teammates' slides. I limit each slide to only one thought, one fact, and one emotion I want the audience to feel! My slides are simple and elegant. It is my job as the innovator to tell the idea's story; my presentation's only job is to create a cognitive anchor* to help remember the story I am telling.

*Note: a "cognitive anchor" is any tool that helps people to remember something.

As it stands now, innovators like Elon Musk, who has kept his companies acting and thinking like a startup, have the advantage in innovation. Some of that advantage comes from the personal experience of entrepreneurs, but much of it can be traced to the poor decisions that many large corporations have made when it comes to how they organize their innovative teams. These problems don't have to be permanent, but if large companies want to regain the competitive edge from their startup competitors, then they need to understand exactly how entrepreneurs think.

CHAPTER 5

HOW
ENTREPRENEURS
THINK

We once read books, then moved on to blogs in the early days of the internet. Now, we're satisfied with reading tweets. We once listened to full-length albums, then moved on to singles. Now we listen to song samples on TikTok that are only seconds long. Letters shrank to emails, and emails have become texts. Everyday experience reinforces the idea that we should think about life in terms of smaller and smaller chunks. The corporate world reflects this trend as well.

They used to focus on building sound companies, then they focused on products, and now they celebrate a new feature of a product that might impress the shareholders. The idea of incremental progress dominates boardrooms today, and corporate investors reinforce it at every turn.

This increasingly incremental prioritization, at the board and executive level, invades the way all people within the organization think about innovation. The typical corporate mindset is based on incremental thinking. Bite-sized innovations seem more appealing to the corporate mind, but it's not going to get the job done. Sure, a small improvement might help achieve your next bonus and appease the shareholders this quarter, but eventually a REAL innovation will be needed for the company to survive. Successful entrepreneurs aren't interested in making slow, steady progress, like corporate competitors. They know that in order to stay ahead of ever-changing evolution, innovation needs to make large leaps into the future. Corporations, meanwhile, are less willing to put the weight of their resources behind ideas that are big enough to be transformative. The good news is that changing this reality merely requires a shift in psychology. If corporate teams can understand how entrepreneurs think, then they have a chance to set themselves apart and build an amazing future for everyone.

NO "I" IN "TEAM"

A common problem in corporate environments is that teams are emphasized over individuals. They become so obsessed with the efficiency of the machine that the individual is erased. Any individual is seen as a component of a larger team and as interchangeable or easily replaced. This toxic system starts to permeate the business, discouraging the most creative employees. They believe completely in a catchphrase that adorns their motivational posters: "There is no 'I' in 'team.'"

There may not be an 'I' in "team," but there is an "I" in "innovation." It's a concept that bears remembering: *Innovation starts with an I*. Every idea in existence started in *one* person's brain. It doesn't start in a team of brains. It's healthy to celebrate the individual. It encourages them and gives them skin in the game when it comes to seeing their idea through to the end. That doesn't mean that teamwork isn't important, but it does mean that credit should be given for the genesis of an idea.

I've been in corporate innovation sessions when they attempt to ideate as a team. Everyone writes ideas on a color-coded piece of paper that they stick on the wall. Once they have enough ideas, they start to vote on the best ones. They build a consensus around the "best idea," but what they end up with is a handful of mediocre ideas that *everyone* agrees with.

When I'm invited to participate in this process, I write my ideas on the Post-it notes and sign my name at the bottom of each one. When it's time to stick the notes on the wall, it never fails that the external innovation consultant running the meeting says, "Oh, no. You can't put your name on these." I ask why not, and the answer is that it's a group exercise. My insistence on adding my name can create a bit of friction in these meetings, but it's something I feel strongly about. When corporations create a culture where individuals are disconnected from their ideas, they end up with watered-down innovation. Entrepreneurs want credit for their ideas, and they accept the risk of failure at the cost of that recognition. People want to follow the ideas that they come up with; they want to go along for the ride. They want to celebrate if they succeed. If you create a culture where you're not rewarding the individual for the brilliance of their brain, they turn that inner brilliance to outside projects. This is universal in every company I've worked with. When I interview the actual innovation team, I interact with them and get to know them personally. And every time what I find is that they're working on more interesting things in their personal life than in their business life. They're not invested in their work because they're not allowed to feel the kind of passion about their work projects that they get to feel about their personal projects.

They have the entrepreneur's mentality, but the corporate environment pushes it away. An enormous amount of innovative energy is simply wasted. Corporations can learn to harness that unused energy by celebrating individual achievement. Instead of making all ideas anonymous, they should allow their most creative employees to become publicly tied to their idea that it can become a part of their corporate identity.

Many of the corporate problems with innovation stem from the fact that they don't understand what motivates and drives the entrepreneurial mind. In this chapter, I'll lay out some of the essential aspects of the entrepreneur mentality. The sooner the corporate world accepts and internalizes this mentality, the sooner they will begin to solve their problems with innovation. Remember, the megacorp you work for was once an idea in one person's mind, which then became a startup. Every corporation was once a startup created by an entrepreneur.

10X VERSUS 10 PERCENT

I have already described the difference between thinking big and thinking incrementally. One way to think about it is that entrepreneurs are always thinking about getting ahead of evolution, while corporates think about how to *respond* to evolution in small, incremental steps. In general, true innovators think about growing at an exponential rate, or 10x, while operators aim for an incremental rate of change, or 10 percent.

Obviously, it's impossible to respond to every little change that happens. Whether it's your personal life or in a business, there is a cost to responding. It takes time, talent, and treasure. Not only is responding to evolution in incremental steps slower, it's also inefficient. But there is another aspect that people might not realize: It's human nature to respond in larger steps. When you think about the changes in the seasons versus the changes in the weather, you find that humans look forward to seasonal changes, but they hate the changes in daily weather. There's something positive about looking forward to winter or summer. You're allowed to let your hopes take over. And as we've seen, hope is a big ingredient in innovation. Changes in daily weather are more annoying, and if we get wrapped up in those small changes, they dominate our thinking.

On the other hand, "10x" thinking is all about unlocking the part of us that looks forward to the exponential change over the incremental. Our educational system and our corporate structures reinforce the idea that incremental change is best, and it can be difficult to overcome their influence. But great innovators know intuitively that the big ideas are the ones that they will respond to with more passion.

SCARCITY BREEDS CREATIVITY

Most of the time the best ideas are built in a state of scarcity. Not having access to everything forces you to rely on creativity, and the truly creative solutions are the ones that are more likely to explode. Whenever I travel, I look for the scrappy ways that people are responding to change in the world. The innovative solutions that people come up with on a shoestring budget are incredibly impressive.

The scarcity of resources was the environment that an amazing innovation called the *Hippo Roller* was created. Over 2.1 billion people suffer from a scarcity of safe drinking water.[8] In Africa alone, one in three people lack access to the most basic of water sources such as wells or taps.[9] Women and children are forced to carry five-gallon buckets of water, weighing forty-one pounds, balanced on their heads for hours a day. Then the most amazing, and in retrospect obvious, solution was created.

Two innovative minds took a 24-gallon barrel, placed it on its side and attached a handle for steering. This incredible innovation now enabled 24 gallons of water to be "rolled" by a single person, over rough terrain, quickly and easily. This idea was brought to life, not by huge NGOs or by a large team

8 World Health Organization, "2.1 Billion People Lack Safe Drinking Water at Home, More than Twice as Many Lack Safe Sanitation," news release, July 12, 2017, https://www.who.int/news/item/12-07-2017-2-1-billion-people-lack-safe-drinking-water-at-home-more-than-twice-as-many-lack-safe-sanitation.

9 Leo Holtz and Christina Golubski, "Addressing Africa's Extreme Water Insecurity," Brookings, July 23, 2021, https://www.brookings.edu/blog/africa-in-focus/2021/07/23/addressing-africas-extreme-water-insecurity/.

sponsored with millions from a corporation. It was created by two people, with scarce resources, who saw the problem firsthand and wanted to help. Like all great innovations the *Hippo Roller*, once released into the wild, was further innovated on by its customers. The *Hippo Roller* is now also used as a cart to carry goods, a roadside stand to sell goods, and a stretcher to carry the injured. Once people saw its utility, they expanded even further. The *Hippo Roller* is also used as a firefighting tool and as a small-scale garden irrigator through the inclusion of an innovative hand-pump that requires no external power. A whole ecosystem of innovation not created through abundance, but from scarcity.

The *Hippo Roller* is the perfect model of innovation in scarcity. What I love about it is the collaborative nature that sprung up because of it—entrepreneurs sharing ideas on how to leverage it with other entrepreneurs. The end-users did not let lack of time, talent, or treasure stop them from solving problems beyond that of carrying water. As a community of like-minded, scrappy entrepreneurs, they expanded the *Hippo Roller* into a variety of other uses. No long meetings searching for consensus. No highly skilled technical staff. No expensive multi-variant testing and focus groups. The creators and users of the *Hippo Roller* had problems to solve. Because they had no choice but to operate in scarcity, they tapped into their creativity and just solved the problem. No corporate MBA's were needed to make it a life-changing success.

We often have too many choices. Abundance creates decadence. Corporations have so many resources in terms of time, talent, and treasure. But if you have too much of any one of those things, you get mediocrity. I have seen corporate innovation teams focus so much on their abundance that they choose to make their teams bigger, or believe they have all the time in the world, or spend insane amounts of money all because they feel they *can*. The decadence I see within corporate innovation teams is truly remarkable. In my experience there's a magic ratio of time, talent, and treasure, and it leans more towards scarcity than abundance. So, the fewer people involved, the fewer dollars available, and a finite amount of time will typically create better, more topical ideas to the evolution that's happening.

The corporate mindset is to always add *more*. They want to spend more time on a project, more time constructing a plan packed with more details, and lamenting how they need more funding to be successful. But the corporate culture of abundance gets in the way of true innovation. Companies who want to succeed at innovation should spend less time planning and learn to move faster with less money. They should embrace the entrepreneur philosophy, and learn how to be scrappy. When they do, things start to happen more quickly, and their ideas improve as well.

THE TWO-HUNDRED-HOUR RULE

There's a danger in spending too much time attempting to develop an idea. Bearing this in mind, it's a good idea to have some sort of limit on how far you go with an innovative project before you sit back and honestly assess how much of a chance it has to succeed.

When I have a credible claim to have an idea that is worth pursuing, I anoint it and give it 200 hours of my time. I keep track of the time closely. The 200 hours starts from the minute I say "I believe, let's go." Every second I think about the new project, I track it. Anything I do related to it gets tracked.

In 200 hours, I personally can flush out a product, create a pitch deck, lay out financials, create a prototype of the final product, and pitch it to some potential customers. I am a "full-stack" entrepreneur with every skill from idea to first customer sale.

After 200 hours, the idea is judged as either a winner or a loser. Within 200 hours I should be able to create some traction by getting someone interested in buying it as a customer, or investing, or interested in joining the project. By 200 hours, I have shared what I have so far with twenty to fifty people to see if there's any spark there. When 200 hours arrives, I take a look at everything and re-evaluate. Some projects really don't generate interest until the last five hours or so.

If there's no traction for the idea, I kill it. I kill a lot of projects, and that's just part of the process when it comes to innovation. Failure is going to happen. It is supposed to happen a lot. It shouldn't necessarily be celebrated, but it shouldn't be avoided as it is inevitable. Failure is part of the innovation process. Show me an innovation team that is not failing, and I will see a team that is not innovating. A lot of companies make the mistake of not killing projects, or they don't have a process to kill them off if they aren't working. They should adopt the 200-hour rule, or at least make a version that fits their business. It could be a thousand hours or ten thousand. But there should be a cut-off point. Not only does that prevent wasting resources on poor ideas, but it forces the people working on the project to focus. The discipline created when you force people to create traction for an idea within specific parameters focuses them to go out into the world to find traction.

TELLING BETTER STORIES

We learn about our history from stories, and stories define our future as a species. Humanity developed around stories, so it's simply human nature to respond to them. I spend a lot of time teaching corporate innovators how to tell better stories. It's really hard to say no to a story you are emotionally invested in. What great innovators understand is that stories and innovation get a lot of their power from the same idea—the unknown. We always want to know what will happen next. How will the plot unfold?

The unknown can be fearful, but it's also exciting. The best stories—and the best innovations—tap into the excitement associated with the unknown. Like storytellers, it's the innovator's job to build a path to the unknown, and through it. All innovation is a story, and an innovator must build upon the story and make it clearer as it goes.

Corporations would rather think about things that have already been done and based upon facts. They shy away from the unknown which by its very nature has zero facts. They want every last detail answered before the project gets started. They don't realize that the innovation process is also a process of discovery. Entrepreneurs know that as the story develops, they will learn things. This is why corporate minds tend to watch what others are doing, and copy the ideas that work. And then they wonder why their products are mediocre. It's because somebody else took the risk, and somebody else believed in the story. Some other executive team bought into a vision, and the story of that vision, without all the "facts." The story itself was funded and allowed to grow into something great. If you will only fund based on facts, then you are not funding innovation; you're funding a copy of someone else's innovation.

The boardroom is such an analytical place that they often forget how powerful emotional storytelling can be. It's powerful because it's personal. And the story I'm about to tell you is a good example of that. I've seen soulless venture capitalist types grow a soul on the spot in response to it.

MY FAVORITE PROFESSIONAL MOMENT

I got up and walked across the restaurant and kneeled down next to an inconsolable six-year-old boy. It was very uncharacteristic of me, normally being someone who doesn't get involved in the lives of random strangers, but I couldn't let what happened to me happen to that kid. I pulled out one of my business cards, looked at his mom and apologized for interrupting. I said, "You don't know me, but I think I can help your son." She looked at me with confusion and fear, weary from the day's events. I could see she was at her wit's end. She nodded silently.

I turned to the boy and told him I owned a magic sticker company.

"Really?" he asked.

"Yeah, I make magic stickers, and I think I can make some stickers to help you fit in better at school. And if you allow me to, I'll make you a set of stickers and send them to you. I think they'll help."

Skinit had been profitable from the day we launched, and about a year in, I had been busy juggling the corollary of our hockey stick growth pattern. It was a Thursday afternoon in August, and I was picking something up to eat at a local fast-food restaurant when I heard five minutes of a conversation between this single mom and her distraught young son which had broken my heart. Mom had just picked him up from his first day of school, and he had *hated* it because the other kids had picked on him.

It transported me instantly to my first day of school, which I remember so purely. I had a slew of medical issues as a young child, and I didn't get to interact with other kids that much. I had lived in a world of books and couldn't wait to go to school. For me, school was this mystical place where I would learn from teachers all the things I had been reading in books. I was so excited on that first day, but like this boy, I was picked on, made fun of, and ostracized. I was watching this replay in my adult life: I was watching *me* in that little kid in line for five minutes.

///

The mom is looking at me like I'm crazy. I take my pen and tell her that if she writes their address, I will ship her son some stickers. She looks at my card and sees the company name: *Skinit—Consumer Electronic Personalization.* She turns my card over and writes down the address, and hands it back. No names.

I look at the kid and say, "Okay, I'm going to go make you some magic stickers, and all I need you to do when you get these stickers is *believe* that they are magic." The kid perks up. He was getting some stickers, and that was good news.

I left, without even going back to get my food. That card was going to end up being something that would change my life. I went back to the office, a factory that made custom cut stickers for cell phones in the identity of the owner to make a device as individualized as the person who possessed it. By that time, everyone had left for the day and it was just me.

I sat down and got to work, setting out to create a stack of *magic* stickers.

I put myself in the mind of a six-year-old and thought about all the things I would like to have on a set of stickers. I picked all kinds of sports teams—Denver Broncos, the Nuggets, Colorado Rockies, Disney content—whatever I could think of. I ended up with about two dozen stickers and sent them to the printing machines, laminated them, then sent them to be cut out. That took a bit of time, and it was getting later into the evening. Finally, when the process was complete, I packed the cut stickers into an envelope with a business card along with a Post-it note onto which I had written a reminder: *Believe.* Sealed it up, addressed it, affixed postage, and drove to the post office to mail it.

And that was it for me. I didn't think more about it. It was this magical evening where I did some work, mailed it, and forgot about it instantly. The following Monday, late afternoon, my phone rings. I pick it up and she says, "I don't know if you remember me, but you made some stickers for my son." I say, "Oh yeah. How did those work out?" And she says, "You have no idea what you've done."

Instantly my hands start shaking. It was an awful thing to hear. *You have no idea what you've done.* I'm holding the phone. Nervously I ask, "What happened?" "Well, he went to school on Friday, and the kids continued to pick on him. And when he got home, he ran out to the mailbox, and your stickers hadn't arrived. I explained to him that they probably wouldn't come, and he was just heartbroken. Saturday comes and he runs out, and your envelope was there, and I was relieved."

I say, "Did he like them?"

She continues: "He opens the envelope and I see the 'Believe' Post-it note, and I stick it on the fridge. I have your business card, and you sent him so many stickers." I tell her, "Yeah, I didn't know what he liked, and wanted him to have plenty of options."

She tells me that they spread them all out and the table and that she finally understood what I meant by "magic stickers." Her son picked out the Denver Broncos.

Again I say, "What happened?"

"After picking out his favorite, he asked if he could take the rest to show-and-tell on Monday. I wrote a note to the teacher, asking if he could do this, and he was excited to show off his stickers. I dropped him off and went home. I worried all day. And then I went to pick him up and I drove up to the school and he wasn't there. I pulled up and was parked and I didn't see him. I saw all these kids, but I didn't see my son. I got out of the car and was frantic because I didn't see my son." She pauses. "And then I heard his voice."

She had looked over and saw this group of kids laughing and joking. And her son was behind them *in* the group. She didn't see him from the car because he was surrounded by kids. He fit in and he wasn't being made fun of. And everyone was just so accepting of him.

She catches his eye, and he runs over towing another kid. He introduces his new best friend, and the kid says something to her. She breaks down crying on the phone with me. This kid had said, "Man, your son is so cool. He's so lucky. I wish I had diabetes, too."

Those stickers I made that night were for his insulin pump.

When I was in school, I had a speech problem. I lost my hearing as a kid, had multiple surgeries to be able to hear. I learned to talk before I could hear, so I talked differently, and kids made fun of me for it. He was being made fun of because he had to wear his insulin pump and that made him different. He would have to leave class to check his insulin pump every day, and he was ostracized because of this perceived handicap.

When I knelt down next to him that day in the restaurant, I saw the make of his insulin pump, and that night, when I went back to my office, I researched the device. I didn't have a prototype, so I had to do all the work to figure out the custom cuts to be able to *Skinit*. Divine intervention happened because I was able to create the cut path using images I found on the internet and created a perfectly fit skin for his insulin pump. But more importantly, I was able to give that kid a story, a way to camouflage his disability. We went on to cad a ton of medical devices for kids.

When I look back on those days—the day I met them, and that phone call with his mom—it was so impactful to know that this whimsical company I created to camouflage consumer electronic devices would have such a huge impact and in such a unique way. To make a device that would connect my history with a young kid's history and solve for him a problem I couldn't solve for myself makes this my favorite professional moment.

There are many facts in that story. A corporate version of the story would have those facts—the dimensions of the stickers, the chemical composition of the adhesives. Those facts are simply not relevant to the innovative impulse—the mysterious thing inside of us that drives us to build a better world. I have told this story dozens of times, and every time I get at least one person in the audience to tear up. Why? The facts by themselves are unremarkable. But when they are woven together into an emotional story, suddenly we care. Each of us can empathize or sympathize with the little boy and his courageous mom. It is the empathy and sympathy the story elicits that makes the innovation so powerful.

INDIVIDUALISM AND STORIES

I find that as I'm working on an innovation, I'm constantly adding bits and pieces of myself. My fingerprints are all over everything. And that's part of what makes innovation so special and rewarding, not just for me, but for potential investors and customers as well. In the startup realm, I can go in with the team and ask who came up with each idea. Someone will raise their hand and then tell me the genesis story. They take me through the whole thing, from inspiration to realization, linking how one thought led to another. There's always a clear path from the ideation to the present moment.

As a culture, we are fascinated with startup founder stories. Even in movies, we want to see the origin stories of our favorite characters. We want to know the initial spark that provided the inspiration for the great things in their life. In the startup world, founders set the tone and create the culture. They are involved in every decision. In the corporate world, they seem to have forgotten the power of personal stories and of individual passion.

In a society dominated by small bursts of engagement like text messages and Instagram stories, it might be tempting to think small and incrementally. All too often, the corporate mindset is to take advantage of the next small thing rather than to take a chance on creating the next big thing. Once the corporate world embraces the big thinking and emotional narratives associated with entrepreneurs, it will be able to compete with startups by creating a culture of innovation that leads directly to the future.

CHAPTER 6

INNOVATION CULTURES, CORPORATES VERSUS STARTUPS

When it comes to building a culture that is conducive to innovation, the focus on operational excellence by corporations often leaves them unable to actually innovate. A few years ago, I was consulting for a big firm that had just put an MBA in charge of a high-profile innovation project. This guy was good at operations, which made him terrible for this job. In one of my first meetings with him, he went over his plans, telling me that he had everything that we were going to need. "Oh, yeah?" I asked. "What do you *think* you need?" "Well," he said, "we've got a foosball table, a fully stocked kitchen with a ton of free drinks and snacks, and the video games arrive next week."

I asked him what those things had to do with innovation, and he told me he wanted to create a "startup atmosphere." As you can imagine, his tenure over this innovation project didn't last very long. His problem was that he didn't really understand what the startup atmosphere was all about, so he latched onto superficial details that he had read about in some glossy magazine. He didn't understand innovation, and he probably didn't understand foosball either, so he assumed that they shared a connection.

Amenities and perks are nice, but they have zero to do with true innovation. Operators on the corporate side see Innovators as weird and quirky, and they don't get innovation culture. Corporate culture works against real innovation in many ways. Looking to startups for inspiration is a good instinct, but unless large companies make an effort to understand how an innovative startup culture works, and the actual psychology of the founders in it, they're going to get it wrong every time.

What does the right culture look like? First and foremost, new innovation is never regarded as an expense; it's always an advantage.

THE CULTURE OF INNOVATION

I wanted to look at the effects of culture on startups and corporations, so I did the research. I looked at startups funded by venture capital, which is a fairer comparison to their corporate innovation team counterparts. Startups that go through Y Combinator or Techstars get a large amount of mentorship and capital. Over the last ten years, 89 percent of these startups were successful. That's a phenomenal hit rate, and it's pretty good empirical evidence that something magical happens in the startup that doesn't happen in the established corporation.

When I share this data with corporate innovation types, they start to realize that something special is happening in the startup culture. They can feel it. All the cool innovations seem to be coming from small groups of passionate innovators. How is this possible? Corporations should have every advantage, yet the data says they're getting beaten soundly by the upstarts. There are even people who fail in corporate innovation, yet when they leave, they become wildly successful as a startup founder. Why?

A large part of the answer is the culture. A culture that is built on the idea of an individual is more likely to lead to success. The individual is able to organically create an atmosphere based on personal values and attitudes. In startups, even large ones with hundreds of people, you are able to see the individual fingerprints that each team member leaves on the innovations. We even share all the crazy stories of who created what and who solved what problems. In the corporate realm, the values and beliefs that the company aspires to are the result of committee thinking. Corporate culture is an artificially manufactured culture, based upon committee buzzwords chosen because they test well in focus groups. All evidence of the individual is scrubbed out so as to not offend the rest of the team. If values are going to be effective, they can't be arrived at by consensus.

Some companies go even more wrong by hiring an outside "culture consultant" to come in and author the company's culture documents. This task is something that should never be outsourced, and yet companies do it all the time. They select a list of well-tested buzzwords, then vote for the best five or ten. It's no surprise that "Innovation" is often one of these buzzwords. It always scores high. It turns out that everyone wants to be perceived as innovative, but no one wants to act innovatively. The company wants its people to be innovative but based on an operationally derived definition of innovation, not true innovation.

True innovation is nebulous and hard to define, so most companies don't even try. They like the sound of it, but they don't know how to achieve it. They claim to be innovative and then fill their innovation teams with operators. I joke sometimes and say, "As an innovator I believe true innovation is the human response to evolution. MBAs, on the other hand, want to change the definition to the least risky option based on a committee's vote."

PROFIT AND VALUE

In startups, we focus on creating value, not creating revenue or profit—at least not at the start. It's vital to focus on creating value in the early days of innovation. The question we ask ourselves is this: How can we give the customer something of *value*? As the project moves along, things become more operational. At that point revenue and profit become important, but the natural course of innovation moves from value to profit.

Corporations screw this up again and again. They need revenue as quickly as possible, and value gets forgotten. I have tried to point this out to every corporation I have ever consulted with. Work on creating value, and once you have done that, *then* you can ask how valuable it is to your customer and hopefully that amount can be distilled down to profit. I come from a world that concentrates on building cultures based on value creation, so it's strange when I get embedded into companies that have both overt and covert innovation cultures focused solely on revenue creation, or worse, profit creation. Both revenue and profit are important, but at the beginning of the innovation process it can be a distraction. I have seen innovation teams so focused on a certain profit profile that they only innovated to meet it, and missed the chance to surpass it. If this team had been focused on creating value, then they would have seen that by innovating a little more, their end profit profile could have been doubled.

The emphasis on revenue and profit shouldn't be surprising. That's how operators think. They're focused on the day to day, on stability. And nothing says "stability" like a steady revenue stream. The startup culture is built around innovation excellence and creating things of value. Most corporate people don't think that the innovative culture can be effective. They want to be innovative, but they don't want to hire many innovators.

If you take a look at the corporate filings of large innovative companies like Google or Amazon or Nike, you can find out how many people they have working on innovation (sometimes listed as R&D). They have a lot of people in those departments. But the companies that call me in a panic, because they are struggling with innovation, aren't investing in it. They think that great innovations are going to appear organically from a well-staffed operational side. Spending on innovation is seen as a waste because it doesn't provide immediate profits. What's interesting is the number of actual persons tasked with "innovation" within most large corporations is between .001–.01% of all employees. That's only one to ten people per a thousand solely tasked with innovating for a large corporation! Yet the corporate company culture espouses innovation as a priority. I always thought this disconnect was weird. When I talk to corporate executives, they get really nervous when I mention that there are more actual innovators in just a few startup competitors than the huge multinational corporation currently has innovating in-house. Take for example a corporation with 20,000 employees. At most, they will have two hundred people working on innovation projects, but realistically I see maybe a few dozen in +90 percent of the companies I have consulted with. Compare that with just three startups, each with around thirty people on the team. Each and every one of those ninety people (thirty people × three companies) is thinking and acting innovatively. If we scaled this out to all the startups trying to take market share from a large corporation, you can see that the in-house innovation team at most corporations is heavily outgunned. Innovation spend *needs* to be one of the top expenditures at *all* companies and not regulated to a "nice to have" mentality.

Innovation based solely on profitability is extremely difficult. Innovation is an expense, especially finding and hiring the appropriate talent. And there are no guarantees of a return on that expense. Anyone who promises unfailing innovation is lying or is not *really* innovating. Some projects will inevitably fail. Even successful innovation projects will have a pathway of failure behind them. But companies that under-stand and trust the overarching innovative process will see rewards in the long run.

CHANGING THE PROCESS

In large corporations, there's a reverence for established processes, and it sometimes takes considerable inertia to change the way that things are done. Good ideas for change are ignored because "It's in our corporate Bible." Leadership feels no ownership of the current process because the process was likely in place when they arrived. You simply aren't allowed to interfere with the process. This makes sense, since on some level the process must work, hopefully at some time in the past, but the devotion to established processes is one of the reasons why innovation is abysmal in large corporations. They treat their processes as law.

To be more innovative, it is not what a corporation needs to learn; it is what it needs to unlearn that matters.

You've probably experienced this when you've interacted with a large company as an employee or customer. There is usually a simple solution to your problem, but it can't be done because of some rule from 1979. I dealt with this exact problem when I recently had a billing issue. I hadn't been paid by a large company for five months. They informed me that everything had been approved, but the billing department was having trouble with bank wires at the moment. "Okay," I said, "just cut me a check and mail it out." They said they couldn't do it because "That's not the process." And they simply can't change the process.

As an innovator, I like to break rules. I especially like to break stupid rules. I'll tell people in corporations that their rules are stupid, because it's something they need to hear. If they have a lot of inefficient rules or processes, especially when it comes to innovation, those rules act as a tax, cutting into the possibility of successful innovations and future profit.

Efficient startups don't have this tax. They don't have established processes, so they develop processes along the way. A process that doesn't work isn't a disaster, because it can be easily discarded for something better. By remaining fluid and forgiving, startups create processes that are finely tuned to the project that they are trying to build. Startups have the flexibility to chart their own path, which means they can move faster than corporations that have erected their own roadblocks. Additionally, startup processes are constantly being reevaluated. A "rule of thumb" last week might be a hindrance this week. When I was building startups, I used to say, "All rules and processes are written in pencil, not pen, and I have a big-ass eraser that I love to use, so let's make sure any rule is *worth* writing down."

FLAWED INCENTIVES

Corporate culture is political and territorial, and bonus structures are based upon profitability and consistency. The bonus structure is one of the primary reasons that corporations are failing at innovation. A large proportion of people's income is tied to metrics like profitability and consistency, and true innovation involves neither. If corporations want to encourage game-changing innovation, they need to create bonus structures, at least for their innovators, that are compatible with that goal.

In a startup culture, incentives are simple: usually some kind of equity in the company. The innovators share in the success of the organization, which makes them believe more in the projects they are working on. Such an arrangement builds trust and clarifies for employees that what's best for the company is also what's best for them as individuals. The corporate world is based more on individual-aligned compensation. Managers tend to set goals for their employees' personal bonuses, which may or may not be aligned with the company's overall goals. This is where Goodhart's Law comes into play. Goodhart's Law states, "When a measure becomes a target, it ceases to be a good measure."[10] I have

---

10   Will Koehrsen, "How to Mind Goodhart's Law and Avoid Unintended
     Consequences," Built In, October 19, 2021, https://builtin.com/data-
     science/goodharts-law.

had corporate executives who have met their yearly bonus goal early tell me that they then "coast" the rest of the year so as to "not increase the goal for next year's bonus too much."

When you put a bonus on the table, people tend to become shortsighted, and in innovation, we cannot be shortsighted and expect to be successful. We have to account for where we're going and the destination we're trying to reach. When leadership creates a bonus structure and includes some metric for which employees earn a large chunk of their compensation, it creates a situation where people subconsciously don't want to risk their bonuses on trying something new. They focus on the proven metrics that will get them their bonus at all costs. And most of the time they need short-term success to get their bonus. Everything becomes about achieving the metric that creates wealth for themselves.

This is a terrible environment for innovation. You might have ten people on the same innovation team, but pulled from different departments, all with different bonus structures and corresponding metrics that satisfy those bonus structures. In a startup that uses equity in the final product as an incentive, everyone works toward the same goal. But in corporate teams, everyone is being compensated differently. They are usually all working on different projects. There's no united theme, no cohesion to the process. In some cases, they are competing with one another because of the individualized nature of their compensation. In the corporate innovation space, it's unheard of for team members to get a percentage bonus based on their individual projects. Human Resources departments usually won't allow this kind of arrangement to happen.

Companies should do more to tailor bonuses and compensation to the innovative goals that they hope to achieve. They should give innovation teams equity, or at least profit-sharing, in their ideas, or to find a way to tie any bonuses to the success of the idea rather than counterproductive metrics like profit or revenue.

ALLOW INNOVATION TO HAPPEN

The startup culture doesn't have the stability of the corporate culture, but in terms of developing employees and making them feel as if they are truly important to the trajectory of the organization, startups have the advantage. This is because employees are much more closely connected to the reality of innovation. I always say that we hire not for the position, but for competency and values. It's common for employees in a startup to not have a set job description. The job and the tasks required to fulfill it are tied to the business map. Startups want people to be where they add the most value. It's a continually changing and evolving "job description" in that sense. In the corporate arena, job descriptions are tightly described and specialized. I have actually had someone on a corporate team tell me, "I am not going to do this. It is not in my job description." But I have also had corporate innovation teammates that have shared that they are "not allowed" to do something that they want to because it is "outside their job description" and that they are not allowed to "play on other people's turf." Creative employees can get locked into positions that don't work for them, and when that happens, everyone suffers.

Individuals push away their natural innovative impulses in the corporate culture. They decide that attempting to innovate just isn't worth it. Since innovation is inherently risky, they stay away from it in order to ensure that they don't lose their jobs. "Why would I innovate?" they ask themselves.

Corporate leadership may say that they want their employees to innovate, but they have created an environment that doesn't allow the expression of the personality traits associated with innovation. They build operationally focused sets of rules and install processes that can't be altered. Rules dominate, no matter what, and creativity is suppressed. But innovators need to know that they can break at least some of the rules. Otherwise, they self discard innovative ideas right from the start.

Startups signal to their employees that it's okay to go against the typical corporate norms, and that's what innovators need to see. That's an environment where wild ideas can be taken seriously so that they can be fairly evaluated. A good example of this can be seen in how the most junior person on a team can challenge the most senior person in the startup. I always smiled internally when a new teammate joined one of my startups and finally felt comfortable challenging me, the CEO & Founder, on a particular idea.

I expect everyone that I bring into my projects to have ideas. I don't just invite input, I solicit it. On their first day, I always tell people that they work *with* me, not *for* me. When people realize that their ideas are seen as valuable, they come up with better ideas because they are encouraged to be curious. All startups create an environment where people are comfortable sharing their ideas. The corporate insistence on rules does just the opposite. "Because I said so" or "That is the way it has always been done" are just two examples I have personally heard that highlight the failure of corporations to truly act innovatively.

HIRING FOR INNOVATION

When you take an operator and tell them to be an innovator, you simply can't expect positive results. Anyone can learn to innovate, but if the traits associated with innovation are not developed and nurtured, you end up with mismatched values. These mismatches occur all the time in the corporate world. If a corporation wants to create a culture that's environmentally friendly, for example, then they should hire people who value the environment. They might ask prospective employees if they recycle. You want people to fit in with the culture that you're creating, and if they don't, it can undermine what the company hopes to accomplish.

With respect to innovation, companies should be asking themselves if they are creating an environment where the traits underlying true innovation are encouraged. Claiming to have an innovative culture is easy, but when I come in, I look to see if that claim is true. One of the hallmarks of innovation is curiosity. Do you allow your employees to be curious? I ask this question of the companies that I work with. They usually answer "yes," but when I look around, I find the same treatment of process as law that I see almost everywhere.

If innovation is important to an organization, then it needs to ensure that it's easy to express the specific traits of innovation. I go through all twenty traits that my research on innovation has identified, and companies can get quite frustrated with me because they begin to realize that they have been using "innovative" as a buzzword. They aren't backing up their talk of innovation with fostering *real* innovation. They aren't doing the work that they must do to install a culture that supports innovation.

Startup cultures have an advantage because they encourage the traits of innovation naturally. The cultures are based upon the founder's values. The innovative person in charge creates a kind of gravity that draws others in, spinning them into the most efficient orbits. Everyone becomes aligned naturally to the innovative impulse, and they all work together toward that collective goal. This doesn't mean that founders are godlike; founders whose values are skewed will create companies that are skewed. We saw this happen with Theranos, a blood-testing startup pitching a supposedly revolutionary technology that turned out to be completely fabricated, where values were compromised. The founder was willing to lie and commit fraud, yet almost everyone underneath her believed that they were a trustworthy company. That's how powerful a founder can be.

When founders and entrepreneurs hire, they look for people who will fit naturally into the innovative plan. Startups hire based on the twenty traits of innovators. Personally, I look for fierce people who have a heartfelt and powerful intensity. I want them to be fierce. When someone attacks their ideas, I want to see them defend those ideas aggressively, with passion. I want them to connect personally with their own ideas and to champion those ideas with ferocity. In the startup world, there are a lot of fierce people. In the corporate world, the fierce people tend to get fired because they can make other people feel uncomfortable. It's much more comfortable to go along with the group consensus on an idea, but that gets you nowhere when it comes to innovation.

Only when the project begins to grow and gets closer to success does a startup look to bring in more operators. The organization hits an inflection point where operational experience becomes necessary. As a result, the culture can change, which can cause its own sort of problems.

Bringing in a foosball table and free food in the kitchen may seem like a way to emulate startup culture, but such actions only illustrate how out of touch corporations are when it comes to innovation. It's not enough to imitate the superficial aspect of startups. If corporations want to catch up to startups, they need to understand how founders think about hiring and culture-building. In the next chapter, I'll describe how to take the best of the entrepreneurial world and apply it to corporate innovation teams.

CHAPTER 7

EFFECTIVE INNOVATION PROGRAMS

deas are like children. Each one is an individual, and each one develops at a different rate. Not all children learn to talk or crawl at the same age. The pace of development can vary widely depending on individual circumstances. Like parents, companies shepherd an idea from conception (innovation) to adulthood (operations) when they are ready to experience the real world. Both people and ideas mature at different rates.

Effective innovation programs recognize that some ideas will get to market more quickly, while others need more time to develop their full potential. There is a process to creating a well-oiled innovation program, but as with any process on the innovative side of an organization, there has to be flexibility for true innovation to flourish. Even innovators can fall into the trap of trying to force a project into a past model of success without considering key differences.

There are no shortcuts to bringing an idea to its full potential, but there are ways to streamline the process. By focusing on a core innovative process that is open to adjustment, corporations can build effective innovation programs that can compete with the scrappiest startups.

ENTREPRENEURIAL/CORPORATE HYBRID INNOVATION

I've talked a lot about how different innovation is between startups and corporations. Most of those differences have to do with psychology and culture. Those differences in mindset and approach can sometimes make people forget that the basics of innovation are true everywhere. The idea life cycle doesn't change based on who is developing the idea.

The idea life cycle works the same way in both venues. Ideas move from the brain to reality in a well-defined way. Here is how I envision an idea's lifecycle:

1. create
2. define
3. research
4. build
5. validate
6. monetize
7. grow

Ideas evolve consistently in both corporations and startups, so it's the environment surrounding this development that matters. Corporate innovation usually attempts to build a template that can fit every project. Of course, what worked for the megacorp a decade ago has no chance of working now. Corporations are obsessed with creating a process of innovation that they can elevate to law. True innovators know that they are not just innovating a product, but also the process that best suits the development of that specific product. Every idea has its own custom recipe—specific ingredients, arranged in a specific way, over a specific time. The only constant is the skills of the innovator.

While the process associated with individual ideas must change depending on the circumstances, the creation of an innovative team is a somewhat formulaic process. You start with people hired for their innovative traits. Then you give them knowledge and train them on that knowledge so they can develop skills. Next you supply them with the appropriate tools that help unlock those skills. When all of that is in place, a team will be able to create the innovation that you're working on.

Innovative teams should be built from the ground up, starting with a solid base of people. As I've noted many times, you want creative people and not operators on this team. The all-consuming focus on operations is exactly the thing that a good innovative team is trying to disrupt. And you don't want to become the thing you're trying to disrupt.

Knowledge is the next area of focus. It's what our innovators will consume, and it becomes the building blocks that they will assemble into the thing that we are trying to innovate. Supplying them with this knowledge is essential, but don't confuse knowledge with facts. The knowledge should be inspirational in nature. It should be focused on creativity. A good test of whether you are providing your innovators with the right kind of knowledge is to consider the kind of media you ask them to read and watch. What magazines, articles, websites, or videos should they be pursuing?

There's a big difference between a TED Talk and CNBC. TED Talks are given by passionate innovators, and they can inspire others to follow wild ideas if those ideas seem valuable. CNBC is concerned with facts and percentages. It provides useful, time-limited information to operators, but it has nothing to offer to creators.

The next step is to train your innovators on the creative knowledge that you supply. Far too often, large companies train their innovators to be better operators, but that will only limit their ability to innovate. When you consider Olympic athletes, it's clear that you want the training to be specialized to their event. When you train them on irrelevant aspects of fitness, you're wasting time that could be spent on skills that apply directly to their specialty. When it comes to training your innovators, don't enroll them in a class on Excel. That kind of operational knowledge is a waste of time for innovators. If you want a team that works creatively, expose them to creative endeavors. Expose your innovation teams to art or other creative pursuits that are adjacent to innovation. For example, I recently helped a client with a video to showcase one of their new innovations. They were surprised that I had deep knowledge of video editing and production. I replied that knowing how to tell stories is paramount for innovators and video is a contemporary way of telling great stories. So why wouldn't I want to know how to do it?

Once your innovators have been given the proper knowledge and training, they can begin to develop skills. The skills of innovation are very specific to innovation, so much so that they can create chaos on the operational side of the business. For example, developing curiosity is crucial for innovators. And the hallmark of a curious person is that they ask a lot of questions. I have spent a lot of time thinking about how questions lead to innovation and therefore I'm known for asking very specific questions and have developed a course that my clients have me teach to their innovators on how to ask good questions.

Asking questions and being curious can cause friction in an operationally focused meeting or group. They can become frustrated with questions very quickly. And for a team consisting of operators focused on operational excellence, it's easy to see why they might get frustrated. They have a process that works, that creates revenue and profit. When I ask questions because I'm curious, they tell me that my questions are outside the scope of the meeting. There are things in the operational world that you don't need to understand in the same way that innovators *must* understand. When you're inventing the future, you have to ask good questions, but too many questions—even good ones—can derail an operational meeting.

As an aside, my question-asking has had an interesting result. Many CEOs love to have me attend meetings because I tend to ask questions that many executives are afraid to ask. Once I lob out a few uncomfortable questions, it greases the skids and the executives in the meeting lose their fear and begin asking real questions themselves.

ENTREPRENEURIAL PROCESSES

There is no set formula for innovation in the entrepreneurial world, but there is still a logical progression that successful innovation teams follow. Much how ideas follow the progression—create → define → research → build → validate → monetize → grow—my own innovative process includes five phases:

1. Ideate
2. Incubate
3. Accelerate
4. Operate
5. Integrate

The Entrepreneurial Process

Phase 0	Phase 1	Phase 2	Phase 3	Phase 4
Ideate	**Incubate**	**Accelerate**	**Operate**	**Integrate (exit)**
Create	Define - Research	Build - Validate	Monetize - Grow	Exit - Integrate
Opportunity Identification and Evaluation	Set Up, Experiment / Learn / Pivot, Proof of Concept	Build, Learn How to Scale	Remove Inefficiencies, Grow Revenue	Full Transition to a Business Unit to Scale or Exit

The skills and traits needed to be successful here...   Are *very* different than the skills and traits needed to be successful here.

Creating a new thing is *much* different than operating it.

The ideation phase is where ideas are created. No idea is too wild not to consider, at least for a little bit. Incubation happens when a promising idea is examined closely through research, experiments, and proof of concept. My team works to define an innovation, and often it begins to change and grow in response to the research being done. Once an idea is defined and showing signs of being

legitimate, it's time to accelerate, to build it out and conduct a lot of experiments as we try to find the perfect market fit. If everything goes well, we reach an inflection point
and begin to bring in operators. We're still not concerned
about profit and revenue, but we do start working on how
to monetize the project. Finally, integration is where the
innovation team parts ways and the project moves on to
integration into a business unit, or an exit into the market
as a standalone venture.

In the corporate world, there are three common frameworks that are used to guide the innovation process: Design
Thinking, Lean Startup, and Agile.

How I Innovate

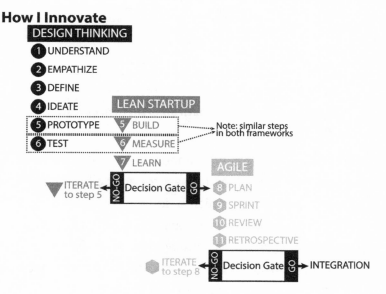

No one on the corporate side ever teaches exactly how these frameworks are supposed to work with one another or why they are supposed to work at all. Put simply, these frameworks are a way of dividing up the five phases. Design Thinking focuses on understanding and empathizing with the customers when it comes to the problems they face.[11] Once these customers' problems are identified and defined, the team ideates on them, creates a prototype, and begins testing it. Once a decision is made to move forward, the idea is plugged into the Lean Startup framework.[12] In this framework, teams test and collect data on the idea. They may go through this process many times until they find a promising market fit. Once a fit is found, the project is put through the Agile workflow, which is a way of planning and scaling up the idea.[13] Teams perform various sprints through the process, then perform a retrospective on each run. They iterate on the agile process until you have something that's really flushed out. Finally, the project is integrated into a business unit, and the innovation team exits.

These are the three common buzzwords in corporate innovation today. And the real problem is that these frameworks

11   Rikke Friis Dam and Teo Yu Siang, "What Is Design Thinking and
  ·   Why Is It So Popular?" Interaction Design Foundation, June 28, 2022,
      https://www.interaction-design.org/literature/article/what-is-design-
      thinking-and-why-is-it-so-popular.
12   "The Lean Startup Methodology Principles," The Lean Startup,
      accessed September 28, 2022, http://theleanstartup.com/principles.
13   "Agile 101," Agile Alliance, accessed September 28, 2022, https://www.
      agilealliance.org/agile101/.

are used individually and are built on top of a host of corporate pathologies. These process politics undermine everything I'm working to build when I'm working inside a large company, which is why I'm a big believer in entrepreneurial psychology and in having teams made up of peers to the executive team that prevent them from messing with this collective framework.

INNOVATION HORIZONS

In any business—in an optimal situation—you have leaders, management, and staff. All three groups have their own "event horizons." Your leaders should be looking years into the future, making big plans. Management should be looking months into the future as they focus on value and revenue on a quarterly basis. The staff then focuses on the day-to-day value and revenue creation. Large corporations have few leaders that focus very far out into the future. This isn't an easy task for operationally-oriented people. They get uncomfortable thinking so far ahead. This is a big problem in corporations today, because it can lead to "innovation theater"—false innovations that don't add any value in the long term. It can also lead to big firms partnering with others solely in the hopes of building a long-term innovation plan. Such partnerships often fail to lead anywhere. A good example of this was the partnership between Walgreens and Theranos.

The management of Walgreens, it seems, looked at Theranos and all the innovation they promised and thought that they had secured a long-term revenue source. But Theranos turned out to be a scam. Corporate teams need a solid team of innovators or an Entrepreneur in Residence (EIR) thinking months and even years ahead. The operational side isn't cut out for it, and the mistakes and lack of planning can be costly. Executives can focus on quarterly reports and stock prices because that's where they are experts. You want your innovators to take over the task of long-term thinking. Asking them to think on shorter timescales only robs a company of the value that those individuals can create.

When you ask your executive operators to think too far out in the future, they don't know how to constructively do so. There is no *real* data for the future yet, and extending trend lines is no better than guessing (or gambling) on longer timescales. What leadership has to do is trust the people who best understand innovation to be able to observe the present and accurately imagine the future.

COVID was an instance of a black swan event that was difficult to predict yet not impossible to plan for. Companies that had invested in creating innovation teams that were trained and skilled to respond to unknown threats responded quickly. Innovators in these companies came in and created amazing solutions and responded quickly to work-at-home and distributed workforce needs. Whether they know it or not, those companies created what I call S.W.A.T. Innovation teams (which I cover in more depth later in the chapter) to respond quickly to immediate needs. This amazing response shows that innovation can have an impact on any timeline if it must.

When it comes to innovation timelines, most companies max out at about three years of foresight. That's about how long it takes for ideas to incubate and make their way to market. Because of the influence of operators, companies tend to think about launching new versions of products they already have. They're not really thinking about the future. Apple's yearly release of the new features of the iPhone is a good example of this. Small improvements are launched on a yearly cadence with a significant product refresh on a four-to-five-year release timeline.

Corporations can't afford to allow their operators to plan their future if they want to extract as much value from innovation as they possibly can. A team of innovative thinkers that is independent of the operational bias is the best way to approach the long-term innovative horizon that can propel a company forward.

INNOVATION THESIS

Companies need to have an innovation thesis, and I often use a template to show exactly what I mean. This thesis needs to be defined in conjunction with your innovation team. There has to be a global thesis that lays out how you build things and how you kill off things that don't fit the thesis. Companies that don't take the time to carefully construct an innovation thesis are going to fail.

Innovation Thesis For _____

"Innovation Program Name"						
Invent We build products with the power to transform the future of _____.			**Incubate** We support new businesses with resources, connections, services, talent, and mentorship.			
Partner We enrich our products and services through mutually beneficial partnerships.		**Invest** We invest in startups that have a high potential to scale and deliver outsize financial returns.		**Acquire** We acquire game-changing companies that can leverage our global reach and resources to bring their innovations to consumers worldwide.		
FOCUS AREAS						
F1		F2		F3		X^{nth}
Enabling Digital Products						
Shared Services and Team						
Leadership	Product	R&D	Marketing	BizDev	Sales	Supply Chain
Operations	Legal	Finance	IT	Creative	PR/Social	HR
iSURF (Innovation Specific Unrestricted Research Facilitation) Separate, _____ S.W.A.T. Innovation team focused on rapidly creating ideas to feed into the _____ Incubate ~ Accelerate ~ Operate process.						

An innovation thesis should be somewhat detailed, but it should also fit on one slide or piece of paper so it can be easily shared and understood. It's good to come up with a name for your thesis, because you want it to have an identity. (For example, Nike's latest innovation thesis is called "Valiant Labs"). Since you also want a visual identity, it's good to have a logo as well.

Below the name comes the focus areas; in this case: invent, incubate, partner, invest, and acquire. These are your innovation strategy components. These components are the tactical areas where your innovation team operates. Depending on the company, some of these areas overlap with the corporate Strategy team's roles and responsibilities. If there is overlap, the Innovation team works in conjunction with Strategy and acts as advisors while "scouting" for opportunities. Beneath that there are focus areas for innovation. In a beverage company, for example, focus areas might be CBD products or non-alcoholic products. Any one focus area might include a large number of possible innovations.

Next on the template is a space for "enabling digital products." Some innovative leads discount this aspect, but I think it's important to clearly lay out what digital products may be created that will help the "Focus Areas" be successful. For example, Twitter started out as an internal tool for software developers to communicate with one another. Next comes the Shared Services Team, listed by departments (this is different for every company). Your Shared Services Team are subject matter experts that can be lent out to the innovation team as needed. It includes different departments such as legal or marketing. Often these shared services teams will be needed for short periods of time or to answer specific questions that arise in the innovation process. Often, they will communicate with the innovation team through one of the enabling digital products. Underneath all of that, I've added an acronym that I came up with—ISURF, Innovation Specific Unrestricted Research Facilitation. This is a separate S.W.A.T.

Innovation team focused on rapidly creating ideas to feed into the incubate, accelerate, operate process.

This is just an example of an innovation thesis. It's one slide that anyone in the organization can read and then be able to understand the philosophy of the innovation team. In my experience, this type of document does not exist in most companies. And yet it is vital in setting out the innovative processes and philosophies that the corporation needs to be successful.

INNOVATION/BUSINESS MAPS

A business map is a simple, elegant way of looking at a business. I created this idea at the very beginning of my career, when I was first hiring people because I wanted them to see how my mind actually sees the business that we are trying to create. I wanted to be able to show them how they fit into everything that we're trying to do. I would take out a piece of paper and start drawing.

Most companies have four main areas: operations, product, marketing, and sales. Everything spins around the operation of the business—the product they are selling; the marketing which creates consumer awareness; and sales, where the product is delivered to the consumer. Within these areas, we have three main skill sets: technological, creative, and relationship. Building a product requires technology. Getting people to notice a product takes creativity. Effective selling of a product means building solid relationships with customers. For most people, this is all standard and obvious.

Business Mapping

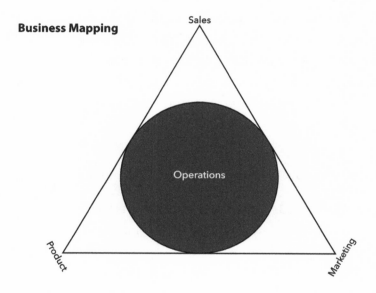

But when we begin to make hybrids between the three outer areas, we find new areas that share skill sets.

For example, halfway between product and marketing we have research and development, which makes perfect sense. Product teams must be creative to come up with new ideas based on what consumers want, but they must also understand the technology in order to know what's possible and what isn't. Between marketing and sales, we have business development, which would include things like the social media team and company partnerships. And between product and sales we have product management, which is where customer service fits in. All of these departments—social media, customer service, and so forth—are adjacent to their outer area, but they lie within the circle of operations. The reason they are within the sphere of operations is because they are more likely to be easily outsourced in a startup.

Business Mapping

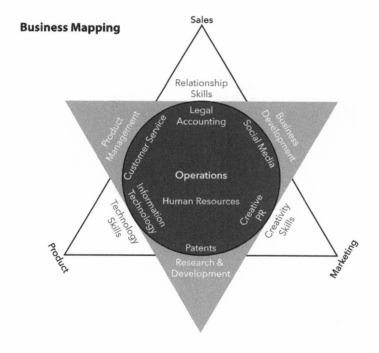

In general, corporations are too focused on the bases of the business map when they should be hiring based on the hybrid roles. They need to focus on "Innovators" (half product, half marketing), "Evangelists" (half marketing, half sales), and "Builders" (half sales, half product). Those are the magic three "personas" that make startups go, because they are hybrids of two different domains, and having one foot in each realm allows them to better see the big picture.

Business Mapping

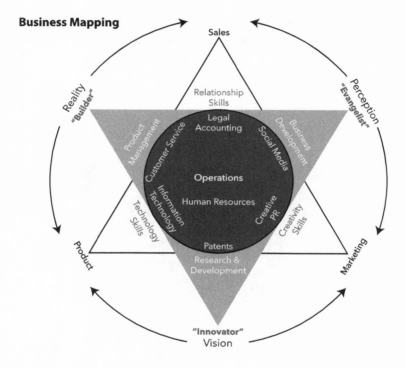

I usually play the role of the Innovator in research and development. Builders take the technology and work with sales to create products that are sellable. An Evangelist works between marketing and sales, and is the persona that spreads the word about the products to both the media and the customer.

Whenever I would bring in a new person to a startup I was working on, I'd show them this map and show them where I saw them fitting in. I can put an X in their spot and use the map to show where my domain is. Not only is the map a good tool to show people where they fit into an organization, it can also help leaders recognize which meetings between groups they need to oversee. For example, I have my "Cross Map" rule of meetings. I never allow my product people to meet with my business development people without me because they are across from each other on the map. If those two groups meet, they might come up with ideas that don't match my strategic goals. They might both decide that they need a partnership with Oracle, for example, while my strategy might be to sell the company to Google. When big-picture ideas are being hashed out, I want to be present in that process. If two teams next to each other want to meet—for example, marketing and product—I can most likely skip that meeting as it will be more specific in nature.

When I explain the business plan to people and show them how useful it is, I can see the light bulbs switch on in their heads. It's the founder's responsibility to set the vision for a company, and the business plan can help that vision become crystallized in the minds of all your team members. When new employees ask me what they should be focused on, I can point to the map, and it's easy for them to understand. It makes perfect sense. For instance, if I'm hiring someone to work in technology, I might ask them to spend 50 percent of the time in their main area and 20 percent in their two adjacent areas. In the case of the technologist, 20 percent in research and development and 20 percent in product management. The last 10 percent can be spread across the rest of the areas, which allows them to be curious in as many aspects as possible. I've done this exercise with marketers and salespeople—everyone on my teams. It resonates with them and helps to define their jobs in a way that makes them more productive and more innovative.

Once I explain this kind of business plan to a company that I'm working with now as a consultant, and they understand more fully how I think about business, then we can create an innovation map. In this exercise, I simply help identify what kinds of subject matter experts they have on hand. These experts could have experience in farming, water resources, energy, environmental science technology—in anything. I'll create subcategories where appropriate; for example, farming experts likely know about machinery, and so on.

Now this company has a good map of its *total* expertise. At this point, we can look at where they are innovating. Almost 100 percent of the time, a new client is only innovating in the center box "Manufacturing & Product." And this makes sense—creating new products for their industry is how companies stay in business. But what is interesting is the companies who have embraced the belief that *all* companies are now tech companies begin to see huge opportunities to build innovations based on their own internal *operational* expertise. The Innovation Map showcases all the realms within the business where they have subject matter experts (SMEs), and in each of these areas they have the ability to innovate as well. When it's mapped out this way, companies can see the experts that they have on hand who are not involved in anything new and innovative. A good example of this is a multinational alcoholic beverage company that I worked with.

Example Innovation Map for an Alcohol Company

Farming	Water	Energy	Enviromental
- Genetics - Machinery - Storage - Vertical	- Sourcing - Filtering	- Wind - Hydro - Solar	- Recycling - Waste
Science	**Technology**	**Finance**	**Legal**
- Chemistry - Microbiolgy	- IT - Automation - Sensors - Data / Insight	- Tax - Commodities - Securities	- Regulatory - FDA - ATF - Politics
Human	**Nonprofit / CSR**	**Operations**	**Transportation / Wharehousing**
- Medical - Consumer - Employee - HR / Recruiting	- Give-Back - Investing	- Ordering - Sales - Accounting	- Mode - Logistics - Distribution
Packaging	**Advertising / Marketing**	**Real Estate**	**Retail**
- Printing - Bottling - Canning - Kegging	- Signage / POP - Digital - Media	- Construction - Development	- Hospitality - Bar / Restraurant - Merchandising - E-commerce
Manufacturing & Products			

When I completed the Innovation Map, I pointed out that they had a lot of experts on government regulation of alcohol, but they weren't innovating in that area. They didn't even know what such innovation could look like. I suggested that they create some kind of software that helps all alcohol companies navigate the complex government regulations on alcohol. It was an idea that hadn't occurred to them because they were solely focused on new product innovation and not processes innovation that could lead to a new technology-based product. They saw themselves as an alcohol company, not a tech company that makes alcohol. I am amazed how many billion-dollar ideas are just sitting within the minds of SMEs within large companies and never worked on because innovation is seen as only for new *consumer* products creation. Your next billion-dollar idea might just be the one that helps all your competitors manage a difficult problem as well as you do.

BUILDING TACTICAL INNOVATION TEAMS

Most companies today are hiring the wrong people to handle their innovation. Meanwhile, startups are overflowing with venture capital and are able to bring ideas to market much more quickly than ever before. The really bad news for big corporations is that the ideas that startups come up with are becoming more and more disruptive. If companies want to reverse this trend, they have to admit that they are struggling with contemporary innovation. They need to augment their standard innovation team with a S.W.A.T. Innovation team to get back on track.

S.W.A.T. is an acronym meaning Special Weapons and Tactics, and S.W.A.T. teams are made up of specially trained police officers with specialized equipment and experience. These teams exist to counter unconventional threats and precarious situations that by their very nature involve high levels of risk and require quick action. They were created due to the increasing "unpredictable" nature of some law enforcement situations. S.W.A.T. teams deal with the non-routine aspects of law enforcement, and they can inflict massive disruption in a small amount of time with a very small team. They are well trained, well equipped, and well funded. S.W.A.T. teams are experienced in fast-moving, high-risk environments. They operate effectively without command overhead, and only the best and most skilled are invited to join. There are many individuals who would make fine police officers but who aren't cut out for the S.W.A.T. team. S.W.A.T. teams are the innovators of law enforcement.

When it comes to corporate innovation I noticed that when I helped companies develop a new, small team that was tasked with "thinking and acting more entrepreneurial," I was helping them create their own internal "S.W.A.T. Team" focused on innovation. Your R&D and standard innovation team is for combatting conventional threats from known competitors. Your S.W.A.T. Innovation team is for combating unconventional threats from unknown or new competitors. In order to build this S.W.A.T. Innovation team, companies must understand the structure and how the team fits in with the rest of the organization. Where is it located? Who does it report to? How do you fund it and are there any legal ramifications? They need to think about oversight and whether the team should have an offensive or defensive strategy for innovation. A lot of these decisions depend on a company's overall innovation strategy.

But one thing that is clear is that the S.W.A.T. Innovation team needs to be somewhat disruptive. It needs to have a culture that differs from the overall company culture because it's focused on doing different things. You need to bring in people who exhibit the twenty traits of innovators, but what skills do you need? Remember, S.W.A.T. stands for "special weapons and tactics" and they exist in police departments to quickly counter unconventional threats. Your S.W.A.T. Innovation teams are not the same as a typical R&D or innovation department, which tends to focus on more conventional threats—primarily known competitors. The S.W.A.T. Innovation team is for combating unconventional threats from unknown or new competitors. This includes startups, which can seem to come from nowhere and develop with breakneck speed. I cover the S.W.A.T. Innovation teams more in my forthcoming book, *Disruptive Innovation!*, coming out in 2023.

Building an effective innovation program based upon entrepreneurial ways of thinking will deliver more successful innovations. When a business is mapped out properly, its employees have clarity when it comes to their role and the expectations for their contributions. As a result, the entire organization is prepared for the changes that evolution brings.

CHAPTER 8

CORPORATE ENTREPRENEUR IN RESIDENCE

L et's do an exercise. Think of the top three innovators that you respect and picture those three people in your mind. My guess is that at least two of the three people you pictured are entrepreneurs. When we think of the top innovators, we usually think of Musk, Zuckerberg, Gates, DaVinci, or Edison. When it comes to innovation, new product creation, the response to evolution—why do we always imagine entrepreneurs?

It's because the entrepreneur is always at the tip of the spear of innovation. Since they don't have the baggage or the legacy associated with typical corporations, they are the most highly optimized individuals when it comes to innovation. They have the freedom to build their team in any way they see fit, unhindered by committee-approved corporate culture and unchangeable processes and rules. Their sole focus is developing an idea that successfully responds to evolution.

As the pace of innovation speeds up, corporations are having a far more difficult time staying relevant. Everything seems to be evolving so fast now, not just in innovation, but in society, in climate, and in technology. These rapid changes are hard to manage in a typical corporate environment. Large companies having the same issues as their large competitors wouldn't be such a big problem, but the rise of startups and the ability for them to take advantage of the plethora of cheap and efficient tools of innovation often leaves the corporate world playing catch-up.

It's not Coke versus Pepsi anymore. It's Coke versus Pepsi and thousands and thousands and thousands of smaller companies spread across the globe. An enormous amount of competition has been unleashed against large multinational corporations. The age of the entrepreneur is upon us, and it's never going away. The tools of innovation are only going to get cheaper, and more talented innovators are going to decide to go into business for themselves instead of working for a large company where they have to navigate antiquated rules that stifle true innovation. Corporations have a tough time figuring out which rules get in the way of progress. Sometimes the rules are covert, and the corporation isn't even fully aware of how they are self-limiting. Because they are creators and innovators, entrepreneurs can see the problems within a corporate culture that will inevitably slow down innovation.

Death by a thousand cuts is happening right now to every entrenched large corporation by the thousands of entrepreneurs who are figuring out how to "unbundle" each and every advantage the company has. Here is a scary exercise I ask potential clients to do. If you are a member of the executive team at a large company, you should ask yourself if you have someone with *real* entrepreneurial experience on your team. If not, it's likely that bringing in an Entrepreneur in Residence, or EIR, could give your organization insight into how entrepreneurial innovators think, how they organize and how they maximize their chances for success.

These EIRs should have a lot of experience on the creator side of the companies they have developed. There are some entrepreneurs who are more operationally focused, but they won't be as helpful. You want someone who has serial successes in coming up with ideas and refining them for the marketplace. The creator persona is often neglected by corporate culture, but they have a lot of insight to share when it comes to the entrepreneurial threats to your business. Trust me, based on my experience in the corporate world, you have *plenty* of MBAs to tap for insight in operational matters. The executive leadership team needs to have someone advising them on the entrepreneurial perspective.

The "in residence" aspect of the EIR is important. Bringing in flyby entrepreneurs to go over documents or spend a day with the innovation team isn't enough. Companies need this valuable expertise to be readily available to their innovators and executives. They need them to be embedded in the culture so they can better identify problems and suggest improvement.

As I've talked about many times, the corporate, operational mode of thought actively works to prevent large established organizations from being competitive against startups when it comes to raw innovation. An Entrepreneur in Residence is a simple yet effective way of allowing executive leadership teams to understand truly innovative thinking so that they can employ it against the many threats all around them.

WHAT AN EIR CAN DO FOR YOUR ORGANIZATION

In order to best understand how an Entrepreneur in Residence might operate within an organization, it's good to look into the specifics. What exactly does the process look like? How can it improve innovative efforts?

In order to explain and define the role of an EIR, such as myself, I created a strategy that I call TAIL:

- **Teach**—I teach executives to "think and act more entrepreneurial" by bringing startup psychology, tools, and techniques into corporate teams. Entrepreneurs have been so successful recently that many of the tools of innovation are calibrated to the entrepreneurial way of thinking. So, in order to best leverage the latest tools, companies need their teams to be fully versed in the entrepreneurial mindset

- **Advise**—I advise by listening to the problems/issues of the company and filter them through my expansive entrepreneurial experience. There is a lot of listening at the start when I take on the EIR role. People understand that I'm trying to solve problems, and so they feel comfortable coming to me and asking for my opinion. They might bring me some data to see what my perspective is, or even ask me about operational concerns. I filter all of this information through my experience with successful (and unsuccessful) companies and give them my honest, informed opinion. Often my opinion isn't what they want to hear, but my "in residence" position within the company reassures them that I'm telling the truth as I see it. I'm not afraid to tell my clients what they don't want to hear, for example, that I know of a startup that has already solved the problem that they're trying to tackle. Most corporate executives tend to discount the small startups, and that's when they get blindsided by a superior competitor. One of my duties as an EIR is to advise them as to which "small" threats they should take more seriously. These large corporations are used to rolling over their smaller competitors. They think they are too big to lose. That may have been true once, but in today's environment, a small team with a focused mission can create a massive disruption in as little as a single year. And corporations are unlikely to see it coming.

- **Invent/ideate**—I take problems/issues and invent/ideate as needed, either with a team or individually, with scarce resources, in risk-prone, high-stress environments. By my very nature, I create things, and so I can help corporations to invent intellectual property. Entrepreneurs are most comfortable creating new things, and in an EIR position they are exposed to a new environment that can ignite their curiosity and lead to inspiration. My experience provides a fresh perspective and "pure mind" on problems that may have plagued a large company for years. And since I'm risk-tolerant, I'm not afraid to propose solutions that have some amount of risk, but which will provide a huge payoff if successful.

- **Liaison**—I take problems/issues and network between teams, departments, or externally. In this role, I can take on any problems within the company and network between internal teams in a way that's different from the executive leadership team. An EIR is able to step outside of the political hierarchy and the turf battles and bring a more collaborative perspective to bear on interdepartmental disagreements.

  - An EIR can act as a glue, sticking teams together in new and different ways. For example, an EIR can identify entrepreneurially-minded subject matter experts within the organization and bring them into the innovation team to inspire them to go out and tackle an audacious problem. In my experience in this kind of position, I've been able to provide different tools or offer a different philosophy.

  - I've especially been able to protect innovators within a company, acting as an insulator to give them freedom to explore their curiosity in a setting that is usually dominated by operational concerns. My experience gives me credibility when it comes to innovation, which allows me to create a layer of protection around the innovators who are attempting to work in high-risk environments. I can help explain and quantify the amount of risk, as well as describe the ramifications of both success and failure. I'll encourage companies to take wise risks, which, in a typical corporate environment, might jeopardize an innovator's career. I help companies understand that if they aren't failing sometimes, then they aren't truly innovating.

○ In addition to being a liaison between internal departments, I can also use my experience and connections to network with the external startup community, from incubators to investors. I speak their language and know their expectations. An EIR can act as an ambassador into the innovative world, probably more effectively than anyone else on the team. I can look at a startup from a different perspective, and I will never trivialize or underestimate a new company just because they are small.

The TAIL acronym not only lays out the specific actions I take once I'm in residence at a corporation. It also serves as a metaphor for the kind of relationship I'm looking to create. Like an animal's tail, I'm somewhat independent and separated from the core, but I'm also connected. EIRs can't be employees. They need to be in residence, but they also need to be external.

Companies can further define the relationship as they see fit. Sometimes they want to keep the EIR hidden from public view. And it makes sense for some companies to want to retain a covert advisor. Others, however, want the EIR to interact with the external innovative community. That kind of relationship makes sense as well. What matters is that an EIR is well connected to the company, yet independent. The other details can be customized as needed.

An experienced Entrepreneur in Residence can be a valuable asset to a company in terms of advice, inventions, and relationships. If more companies consider this approach, they will be better prepared to battle the next disruptive startup.

WHAT TO LOOK FOR IN AN EIR

How do you hire the perfect Entrepreneur in Residence? The first thing to look for is if they have deep, real-world experience building companies. They should be serially successful as well. They don't have to have a 100 percent success rate. That's just not realistic and is a red flag. You want them to be more experienced on the creative side of things rather than the operational side. The point of an EIR is to bring in creative experience. Multinational corporations don't need any more operational expertise.

A prospective EIR should be good at starting, building, and selling businesses. They should be focused on large-scale opportunities. The businesses that I created started small and grew extremely rapidly, and this is the kind of experience that's most helpful when you have problems remaining innovative. A good EIR should understand what it means to create an entrepreneurial-focused business and should be able to give a large amount of insight into what it means to be an entrepreneur and a creator.

At the same time, they should have some experience working with corporations, including understanding the gaps between the startup world and the corporate world. The successful companies that I created always partnered with large multi-nationals when it came to sales. I built white-label technology that they took to their customers, so I worked with a lot of innovation teams over the years. It's incredibly helpful to have someone who has experience dealing with large companies. They come in with an understanding of the political nature of the boardroom and, as such, are able to work through the red tape more efficiently because they've navigated it success-fully in the past. If someone hasn't worked with a large com-pany before, and that person tries to come in as an EIR, they are more likely to create chaos than effective innovation.

Other traits are more obvious. You want someone who has a large network, and that usually comes along with a serially successful entrepreneur. An EIR with experience in mentor-ship is great to have and, in general, you want your EIR to be well respected by other innovators. If they're acting as the public face for your company, you want to make sure they have a good reputation.

THE CONFORMITY EXPERIMENT

My background is in psychology, and there was a famous study from the 1960s that illustrates how important an Entrepreneur in Residence can be to an organization. The experiment is called the Solomon Asch conformity experiment.

The study went like this: The researchers would gather a group of people together around a table and show them a pair of images. The trick was that only one person at the table was a subject of the experiment. Everyone else was working with the researchers, and they were all instructed to give the incorrect answer when asked a question about the images. If everyone was shown two pictures of lines and asked which line was longer, everyone would name the shorter line as the longest. And the subject of the experiment would go along with the obviously wrong answer about 75 percent of the time.

The subjects didn't want to be the only one to give an answer, even though it should have been obvious that they were correct.[14]

This kind of social pressure to go along with the

---

14   Saul McLeod, "Solomon Asch - Conformity Experiment," Simply Psychology, December 28, 2018, https://www.simplypsychology.org/asch-conformity.html.

consensus happens all the time in the corporate world. People shoot down ideas just because everyone else is against them. They value social approval more than being correct, and it's a big problem in a business where the correct answer could be the difference between success and failure.

But the researchers conducting the conformity experiment had one more twist. They wanted to know what would happen if there were another person in the group who stood up for the correct answer, a "true partner." And what they found was that when there was someone else bucking the consensus, subjects were far more likely to stand up for the correct answer. In some ways, an EIR acts as that second true voice that can allow members of a team to become more comfortable and willing to challenge the consensus when they are confident that they're right.

THE DAY-TO-DAY OF AN EIR

My typical engagement as an EIR is usually sponsored by the head of innovation (the Chief Innovation Officer, CINO, if a company has one), the head of strategy (Chief Strategy Officer, CSO), or the CEO/President of the company. My mandate is to help the executive team and company innovators to take the entrepreneurial perspective into account. Simply put, I help the company "think and act more entrepreneurial." Depending on the needs of the company, I work anywhere from two to eight hours a week, with the majority of the time being spent in meetings. As I wrote earlier, I spend a lot of time voicing a very different opinion about the future direction of a company's innovation efforts. It is cheaper in the long run to innovate like a startup from the start versus waiting for a startup to steal market share from you with the result being you then have to acquire the startup for a high multiple.

When I am not in meetings, I am working directly with a company's innovators helping them to move faster, spend less money, and realize a bigger impact in their innovation efforts. I am also "on-call" for anyone on the team to chat about innovation in general. From board members, to executives, to in-the-trench innovators, I have had some fascinating discussions over the years, and have been told frequently how my perspective "opened eyes" on how to compete and win in the contemporary innovation game.

I will close this chapter and the book with the delicate discussion on how much you should expect to pay a corporate EIR. For me it is a balance between how much I can make building another startup as a serial entrepreneur versus how much I can make consulting, writing books, and EIR work. I do love building startups, but I have discovered I love helping corporate innovators be successful more. There are so many resources now to help new entrepreneurs become successful at building their startups. And I participate in a few of these as a mentor. But there is very little support for companies trying to figure out why they cannot innovate at the pace and scale as startups. The people who are advising in the corporate space, the dreaded "innovation consultants," more than likely have zero experience starting, building, and exiting entrepreneurial ventures. Next time your company wants to hire an "innovation consultant," look at their LinkedIn profile and search for real-world, contemporary experience building an entrepreneurial venture. Remember the exercise at the beginning of this chapter? You probably picked entrepreneur innovators as the best, so why would you want to hire innovators without that specific experience?

This brings me to the costs of working with someone like me. I am not inexpensive (my lost opportunity cost), yet I also return a very high multiple on my fee. At the beginning of every engagement I tell my sponsor that along the journey we are going to take together, there will come a moment when I share one thing that will have so great an impact that it either saves the company a high multiple of my overall fee, or I help create something that goes on to be worth a high multiple of my fee. Just one thing I say or do covers my whole fee. This is the precise thing you need to think about and look for in any EIR you are considering. I believe this metric should be what you look for in any "innovation consultant."

CONCLUSION

Most companies suck at innovation, but they don't have to. Now that you understand why companies have lost the war against startups, how they've failed to embrace the culture of innovation, you can get your business back into fighting shape. Your company already has the talent and resources it needs to innovate, and now that you have a sense of what innovation actually is, you can get to work.

The first thing you should do is download my slides at inspirer.com. That presentation is the PowerPoint version of this book. When you're sharing it with your team, you'll be able to fill in the details with what you've learned from reading this book. An even better idea would be to invite me to present my slides directly to your team or to have your entire team read this book.

My website, *inspirer.com*, has a variety of digital resources that you can use to improve innovation at your company. Consider everything I have to offer and see what fits best for your business.

Next, get your entire team assembled and ask some honest questions. Though you might have an inclination of what your company culture encourages and how your business runs, you need to engage your team members. This is what you should ask everyone on your team:

- Does our company culture promote employees to be innovators?
- Are we more focused on operations of the business or innovation?
- How many people in our company are Innovators?
- How many people in our company are Operators?
- What is the company's definition of innovation?

These questions will generate an interesting dialogue, especially when you ask them of the corporate leadership team. In order to chase true innovation in your business, you need to honestly assess where your company is at and how your people feel about it.

Then you'll be ready to bring on an EIR. Once you and your team share a common lexicon of innovation and are ready to get started, you'll be prepared to bring on expertise. You have the talent, the resources, and now the drive to innovate: you just need someone to shepherd that process.

You need fearless disruptive thinking. You need people to break you out of the funk that led you to reading this book in the first place. Hire an ex-entrepreneur, someone who founded and sold a startup or two, or anyone with deep outsider knowledge of contemporary innovation. There is a line out the door of people with the same irrelevant degree eager to work for your company. Each of them will give you the same advice that will send you in the same direction: downward and away from current market trends. Do yourself a favor and look for someone unconventional.

This book is just the beginning of your company's journey toward true innovation, so reach out to me and ask for more details as you need them. We can schedule a call, a corporate workshop, or anything else that would help you and your team. You can also hire my consulting company, Inspirer, for more thorough advice. As an entrepreneur, I want there to be more innovation in the world: I want businesses to stretch farther and take bigger risks.

Write me a review on Amazon or LinkedIn. That's the best way you can help me share this advice and write more of it. I want to hear your thoughts about this book. Innovation is hard work, so if this book helped you be a more innovative business or helped you compete with the thousands of startups out there, I want to know about it.

True innovation is within your grasp. You already have everything you need to do it. I believe everyone is an innovator; everyone has it in them to take something out of date and adapt it to a new environment. Tap into that most essential part of the human experience and you'll take your company to the next level. Innovation is humanity's birthright—and now you're ready to create what's next.

ABOUT THE AUTHOR

MIKE STEMPLE

Mike has built over twenty startups, is an expert at ideation, innovation, and startup psychology, and advises corporate executives on how to "think and act more entrepreneurial." As an entrepreneur, Mike's most notable company exits include SkinIt and Original Wraps (bought by 3M). Mike spends his time now writing books on innovation and promoting the use of Corporate Entrepreneurs in Residence, a position he pioneered. He has taught over 15,000 students from 149 countries on how to build successful startups. Mike has mentored at Techstars and Founder Institute, is an ex-ultrarunner, a semi-famous sports artist, and a veteran of the United States Army. Most days, Mike can be found wearing a t-shirt, shorts, and flip-flops, listening to Jimmy Buffett while watching his beautiful wife surf from the comfort of his oceanview home, as he pets his dog, and pontificates on all things innovative. Mike can be reached on LinkedIn, through his company Inspirer, or at mike@inspirer.com.

CAREER HIGHLIGHTS

- 2001—Built the world's first Bluetooth-delivered multimedia application for handheld personal digital assistants (PDAs).

- 2002—Built the world's first location-based, Wi-Fi–delivered, streaming video solution to mobile devices (PDAs) utilized by Blockbuster Entertainment retail locations.

- 2003—Built the world's first app store platform for delivery of mobile applications and content, utilized by Maxim, Tiger Beat & Bop Magazines, Sobe Beverages, America's Top Model, Best Buy, RadioShack, among others.

- 2003—Built the world's first PIN Card (gift card) for mobile content redemption through online ecommerce.

- 2004—Built the world's first mobile content vending machine utilized by RadioShack and Best Buy.

- 2004—Built the world's first large-scale personalization platform for consumer electronics utilized by a who's-who of consumer electronic companies and wireless carriers.

- 2006—Built the world's first large-scale platform for vehicle personalization utilized by the majority of automotive manufacturers and bought by 3M.

- 2006—Built the world's first large-scale platform for sport accessory personalization utilized by the top water bottle manufacturers.

- 2008—Built the world's first auto content aggregation to mobile device solution.

- 2009—Built a platform to tackle the problem of allowing parents to monitor their kids' social media for inappropriate content.

- 2011—Aided a well-known mobile phone company with their Bluetooth LE Drivers for the next generation of smartphones.

- 2011—Built the world's first Bluetooth low-energy accessory solution for smartphones.

- 2013—Built and launched a successful Kickstarter for a new type of mobile device case.

- 2014—As a consultant, built an innovative wireless ankle monitor (Confidential Project).

- 2015–present—As a consultant, built numerous large-scale innovations that are currently under NDAs.

CPSIA information can be obtained
at www.ICGtesting.com
Printed in the USA
BVHW041947231122
652684BV00001B/29